Flask Framework Cookbook

Over 80 hands-on recipes to help you create small-to-large web applications using Flask

Shalabh Aggarwal

[PACKT] open source
PUBLISHING   community experience distilled

BIRMINGHAM - MUMBAI

Flask Framework Cookbook

First published: November 2014

Production reference: 1151114

Published by Packt Publishing Ltd.
Livery Place
35 Livery Street
Birmingham B3 2PB, UK.

ISBN 978-1-78398-340-7

www.packtpub.com

Cover image by Pratyush Mohanta (tysoncinematics@gmail.com)

Credits

Author
Shalabh Aggarwal

Reviewers
Matt Copperwaite
Christoph Heer
Jack Stouffer

Commissioning Editor
Ashwin Nair

Acquisition Editor
Subho Gupta

Content Development Editor
Amey Varangaonkar

Technical Editor
Taabish Khan

Copy Editor
Karuna Narayanan

Project Coordinator
Leena Purkait

Proofreaders
Simran Bhogal
Paul Hindle
Maria Gould
Ameesha Green

Indexer
Mariammal Chettiyar

Production Coordinator
Arvindkumar Gupta

Cover Work
Arvindkumar Gupta

About the Author

Shalabh Aggarwal has several years of experience in developing business systems and web applications for small-to-medium scale industries. He started his career working on Python, and although he works on multiple technologies, he remains a Python developer at heart. He is passionate about open source technologies and writes highly readable and quality code. He is a major contributor to some very popular open source applications. He has worked with Openlabs Technologies and Consulting (P) Limited as the CTO for a large part of his career. He is also active in voluntary training for engineering students on nonconventional and open source topics.

When not working with full-time assignments, he consults for start-ups on leveraging different technologies. When not writing code, he writes non-technical literature and makes music with his guitar.

I would like to dedicate this book to my late father who will always be there in my thoughts for the love and encouragement he gave me to explore new things in life. I would like to thank my family, my mother and my sister, for putting up with me during my long writing and research sessions. I would also like to thank my friends and colleagues who encouraged me and kept the momentum going. I would like to convey deep gratitude to my mentor, Sharoon Thomas, who introduced to these technologies and helped me learn a lot. Without the support of all of them, I would have never been able to learn these technologies and complete this book.

About the Reviewers

Matt Copperwaite graduated in Computer Systems and Networks with a BSc Hons degree from University of Plymouth in 2008 and has since worked in the private and public sectors in the UK. He is currently a Python software developer and DevOps engineer for the UK government, mostly working in Django. However, his first love is Flask, using which he has built several products, all under the GPL license.

Matt is also a trustee of South London Makerspace, a hackerspace-like community in south London. He is a co-host of The Dick Turpin Road Show, a podcast about free and open source software, and the LUG "Master" of the Greater London Linux User Group.

> I would like to thank my fiancée, Marie, who has put up with my crazy ideas and always makes me laugh, and my parents, who afforded me all the opportunities to get into computing and for their unconditional love.

Christoph Heer is a passionate Python developer based in Germany. He likes to develop web applications and also tools and systems for infrastructure optimization, management, and monitoring. He is proud to be part of the great Python community and wishes to have more time for open source contribution.

Currently, Christoph is studying Computer Science in Karlsruhe in cooperation with his current employer, SAP, and is going to finish his degree in the fall of 2015.

> I would like to thank Armin Ronacher for his work for the Python community, especially for Flask and his inspiring API designs and well-written documentation.

Jack Stouffer is a web programmer from the Metro Detroit area. He works for Apollo America. At Apollo, he creates various web applications using Python, Flask, and Backbone.js, which manage everything from KPI tracking and display to controlling manufacturing. He is currently attending college at Oakland University in Rochester, Michigan.

www.PacktPub.com

Support files, eBooks, discount offers, and more

For support files and downloads related to your book, please visit www.PacktPub.com.

Did you know that Packt offers eBook versions of every book published, with PDF and ePub files available? You can upgrade to the eBook version at www.PacktPub.com and as a print book customer, you are entitled to a discount on the eBook copy. Get in touch with us at service@packtpub.com for more details.

At www.PacktPub.com, you can also read a collection of free technical articles, sign up for a range of free newsletters and receive exclusive discounts and offers on Packt books and eBooks.

http://PacktLib.PacktPub.com

Do you need instant solutions to your IT questions? PacktLib is Packt's online digital book library. Here, you can search, access, and read Packt's entire library of books.

Why Subscribe?

- Fully searchable across every book published by Packt
- Copy and paste, print, and bookmark content
- On demand and accessible via a web browser

Free Access for Packt account holders

If you have an account with Packt at www.PacktPub.com, you can use this to access PacktLib today and view 9 entirely free books. Simply use your login credentials for immediate access.

Table of Contents

Preface

Flask is a lightweight web application microframework written in Python. It makes use of the flexibility of Python to provide a relatively simple template for web application development. Flask makes it possible to write simple one-page applications, but it also has the power to scale them and build larger applications without any issues.

Flask has excellent documentation and an active community. It has a number of extensions, each of which have documentation that can be rated from good to excellent. There are a few books also available on Flask; they are great and provide a lot of insight into the framework and its applications. This book tries to take a different approach to explain the Flask framework and multiple aspects of its practical uses and applications as a whole.

This book takes you through a number of recipes that will help you understand the power of Flask and its extensions. You will start by seeing the different configurations that a Flask application can make use of. From here, you will learn how to work with templates, before learning about the ORM and view layers, which act as the foundation of web applications. Then, you will learn how to write RESTful APIs with Flask, after learning various authentication techniques. As you move ahead, you will learn how to write an admin interface followed by the debugging and logging of errors in Flask. You will also learn how to make your applications multilingual and gain an insight into the various testing techniques. Finally, you will learn about the different deployment and post-deployment techniques on platforms such as Apache, Tornado, Heroku, and AWS Elastic Beanstalk.

By the end of this book, you will have all the necessary information required to make the best use of this incredible microframework to write small and big applications and scale them with industry-standard practices.

A good amount of research coupled with years of experience has been used to develop this book, and I really wish that this book will benefit fellow developers.

What this book covers

Chapter 1, Flask Configurations, helps in understanding the different ways in which Flask can be configured to suit various needs as per the demands of the project. It starts by telling us how to set up our development environment and moves on to the various configuration techniques.

Chapter 2, Templating with Jinja2, covers the basics of Jinja2 templating from the perspective of Flask and explains how to make applications with modular and extensible templates.

Chapter 3, Data Modeling in Flask, deals with one of the most important part of any application, that is, its interaction with the database systems. We will see how Flask can connect to database systems, define models, and query the databases for the retrieval and feeding of data.

Chapter 4, Working with Views, talks about how to interact with web requests and the proper responses to be catered for these requests. It covers various methods of handling the requests properly and designing them in the best way.

Chapter 5, Webforms with WTForms, covers form handling, which is an important part of any web application. As much as the forms are important, their validation holds equal importance, if not more. Presenting this information to the users in an interactive fashion adds a lot of value to the application.

Chapter 6, Authenticating in Flask, deals with authentication, which sometimes acts as a thin red line between the application being secure and insecure. This chapter deals with social logins in detail.

Chapter 7, RESTful API Building, helps in understanding REST as a protocol and then talks about writing RESTful APIs for Flask applications.

Chapter 8, Admin Interface for Flask Apps, focuses on writing admin views for Flask applications. First, we will write completely custom-made views and then write them with the help of an extension.

Chapter 9, Internationalization and Localization, expands the scope of Flask applications and covers the basics of how to enable support for multiple languages.

Chapter 10, Debugging, Error Handling, and Testing, moves on from being completely development-oriented to testing our application. With better error handling and tests, the robustness of the application increases manifold and debugging aids in making the lives of developers easy.

Chapter 11, Deployment and Post Deployment, covers the various ways and tools using which the application can be deployed. Then, you will learn about application monitoring, which helps in keeping track of the performance of the application.

Chapter 12, Other Tips and Tricks, is a collection of some handy tricks that range from full-text search to caching. Then finally, we will go asynchronous with certain tasks in Flask applications.

What you need for this book

In most cases, you will just need a computer system with an average configuration to run the code present in this book. Usually, any OS will do, but Linux and Mac OS are preferred over Windows.

Who this book is for

If you are a web developer who wants to learn more about developing applications in Flask and scale them with industry-standard practices, this is the book for you. This book will also act as a handy tool if you are aware of Flask's major extensions and want to make the best use of them.

It is assumed that you have knowledge of Python and a basic understanding of Flask. If you are completely new to Flask, reading the book from the first chapter and going forward will help in getting acquainted with Flask as you go ahead.

Conventions

In this book, you will find a number of styles of text that distinguish between different kinds of information. Here are some examples of these styles, and an explanation of their meaning.

Code words in text, database table names, folder names, filenames, file extensions, pathnames, dummy URLs, user input, and Twitter handles are shown as follows: "After that, create a new file called `run.py` in the topmost folder."

A block of code is set as follows:

```
MESSAGES = {
    'default': 'Hello to the World of Flask!',
    'great': 'Flask is great!!',
}
```

When we wish to draw your attention to a particular part of a code block, the relevant lines or items are set in bold:

```
from wtforms import FileField

class Product(db.Model):
    image_path = db.Column(db.String(255))

    def __init__(self, name, price, category, image_path):
```

```
        self.image_path = image_path

class ProductForm(NameForm):
    image = FileField('Product Image')
```

Any command-line input or output is written as follows:

```
$ python setup.py install
```

New terms and **important words** are shown in bold. Words that you see on the screen, in menus or dialog boxes for example, appear in the text like this: "Fill up the form and click on **Submit**."

> Warnings or important notes appear in a box like this.

> Tips and tricks appear like this.

Reader feedback

Feedback from our readers is always welcome. Let us know what you think about this book—what you liked or may have disliked. Reader feedback is important for us to develop titles that you really get the most out of.

To send us general feedback, simply send an e-mail to feedback@packtpub.com, and mention the book title via the subject of your message.

If there is a topic that you have expertise in and you are interested in either writing or contributing to a book, see our author guide on www.packtpub.com/authors.

Customer support

Now that you are the proud owner of a Packt book, we have a number of things to help you to get the most from your purchase.

Downloading the example code

You can download the example code files for all Packt books you have purchased from your account at http://www.packtpub.com. If you purchased this book elsewhere, you can visit http://www.packtpub.com/support and register to have the files e-mailed directly to you.

Errata

Although we have taken every care to ensure the accuracy of our content, mistakes do happen. If you find a mistake in one of our books—maybe a mistake in the text or the code—we would be grateful if you would report this to us. By doing so, you can save other readers from frustration and help us improve subsequent versions of this book. If you find any errata, please report them by visiting `http://www.packtpub.com/submit-errata`, selecting your book, clicking on the **errata submission form** link, and entering the details of your errata. Once your errata are verified, your submission will be accepted and the errata will be uploaded on our website, or added to any list of existing errata, under the Errata section of that title. Any existing errata can be viewed by selecting your title from `http://www.packtpub.com/support`.

Piracy

Piracy of copyright material on the Internet is an ongoing problem across all media. At Packt, we take the protection of our copyright and licenses very seriously. If you come across any illegal copies of our works, in any form, on the Internet, please provide us with the location address or website name immediately so that we can pursue a remedy.

Please contact us at `copyright@packtpub.com` with a link to the suspected pirated material.

We appreciate your help in protecting our authors, and our ability to bring you valuable content.

Questions

You can contact us at `questions@packtpub.com` if you are having a problem with any aspect of the book, and we will do our best to address it.

1

Flask Configurations

This introductory chapter will help you to understand the different ways Flask can be configured to suit various needs as per the demands of the project.

In this chapter, we will cover the following recipes:

- ► Environment setup with virtualenv
- ► Handling basic configurations
- ► Class-based settings
- ► Organization of static files
- ► Being deployment specific with instance folders
- ► Composition of views and models
- ► Creating a modular web app with blueprints
- ► Making a Flask app installable using setuptools

Introduction

"Flask is a microframework for Python based on Werkzeug, Jinja2 and good intentions."

Flask official documentation

Why micro? Does it mean that Flask is lacking in functionality or that your complete web application has to mandatorily go inside one file? Not really! It simply refers to the fact that Flask aims at keeping the core of the framework small but highly extensible. This makes writing applications or extensions very easy and flexible and gives developers the power to choose the configurations they want for their application, without imposing any restrictions on the choice of database, templating engine, and so on. In this chapter, you will learn some ways to set up and configure Flask.

Getting started with Flask hardly takes 2 minutes. Setting up a simple Hello World application is as easy as baking a pie:

```
from flask import Flask
app = Flask(__name__)

@app.route('/')
def hello_world():
    return 'Hello to the World of Flask!'

if __name__ == '__main__':
    app.run()
```

Now, Flask needs to be installed; this can be done simply via `pip`:

$ pip install Flask

The preceding snippet is a complete Flask-based web application. Here, an instance of the imported `Flask` class is a **Web Server Gateway Interface** (**WSGI**) (`http://legacy.python.org/dev/peps/pep-0333/`) application. So, `app` in this code becomes our WSGI application, and as this is a standalone module, we set the `__name__` string as `'__main__'`. If we save this in a file with the name `app.py`, then the application can simply be run using the following command:

$ python app.py
  * Running on http://127.0.0.1:5000/

Now, if we just head over to our browser and type `http://127.0.0.1:5000/`, we can see our application running.

> Never save your application file as `flask.py`; if you do so, it will conflict with Flask itself while importing.

Environment setup with virtualenv

Flask can be installed using `pip` or `easy_install` globally, but we should always prefer to set up our application environment using `virtualenv`. This prevents the global Python installation from getting affected by our custom installation by creating a separate environment for our application. This separate environment is helpful because you can have multiple versions of the same library being used for multiple applications, or some packages might have different versions of the same libraries as dependencies. `virtualenv` manages this in separate environments and does not let a wrong version of any library affect any application.

How to do it...

We will first install `virtualenv` using `pip` and then create a new environment with the name `my_flask_env` inside the folder in which we ran the first command. This will create a new folder with the same name:

```
$ pip install virtualenv
$ virtualenv my_flask_env
```

Now, from inside the `my_flask_env` folder, we will run the following commands:

```
$ cd my_flask_env
$ source bin/activate
$ pip install flask
```

This will activate our environment and install Flask inside it. Now, we can do anything with our application within this environment, without affecting any other Python environment.

How it works...

Until now, we have used `pip install flask` multiple times. As the name suggests, the command refers to the installation of Flask just like any Python package. If we look a bit deeper into the process of installing Flask via `pip`, we will see that a number of packages are installed. The following is a summary of the package installation process of Flask:

```
$ pip install -U flask
Downloading/unpacking flask
….........
….........
Many more lines.........
….........
Successfully installed flask Werkzeug Jinja2 itsdangerous markupsafe
Cleaning up...
```

 In the preceding command, `-U` refers to the installation with upgrades. This will overwrite the existing installation (if any) with the latest released versions.

If we notice carefully, there are five packages installed in total, namely `flask`, `Werkzeug`, `Jinja2`, `itsdangerous`, and `markupsafe`. These are the packages on which Flask depends, and it will not work if any of them are missing.

There's more...

To make our lives easier, we can use `virtualenvwrapper`, which, as the name suggests, is a wrapper written over `virtualenv` and makes the handling of multiple `virtualenv` easier.

> Remember that the installation of `virtualenvwrapper` should be done at a global level. So, deactivate any `virtualenv` that might still be active. To deactivate it, just use the following command:
>
> ```
> $ deactivate
> ```
>
> Also, it is possible that you might not be able to install the package at a global level because of permission issues. Switch to superuser or use `sudo` in this case.

You can install `virtualenvwrapper` using the following commands:

```
$ pip install virtualenvwrapper
$ export WORKON_HOME=~/workspace
$ source /usr/local/bin/virtualenvwrapper.sh
```

In the preceding code, we installed `virtualenvwrapper`, created a new environment variable with the name `WORKON_HOME`, and provided it with a path, which will act as the home for all our virtual environments created using `virtualenvwrapper`. To install Flask, use the following commands:

```
$ mkvirtualenv flask
$ pip install flask
```

To deactivate a `virtualenv`, we can just run the following command:

```
$ deactivate
```

To activate an existing `virtualenv` using `virtualenvwrapper`, we can run the following command:

```
$ workon flask
```

See also

References and installation links are as follows:

- https://pypi.python.org/pypi/virtualenv
- https://pypi.python.org/pypi/virtualenvwrapper
- https://pypi.python.org/pypi/Flask
- https://pypi.python.org/pypi/Werkzeug

- https://pypi.python.org/pypi/Jinja2
- https://pypi.python.org/pypi/itsdangerous
- https://pypi.python.org/pypi/MarkupSafe

Handling basic configurations

The first thing that comes to mind is configuring a Flask application as per the need. In this recipe, we will try to understand the different ways in which Flask configurations can be done.

Getting ready

In Flask, a configuration is done on an attribute named `config` of the `Flask` object. The `config` attribute is a subclass of the dictionary data type, and we can modify it just like any dictionary.

How to do it...

For instance, to run our application in the debug mode, we can write the following:

```
app = Flask(__name__)
app.config['DEBUG'] = True
```

> The `debug` Boolean can also be set at the `Flask` object level rather than at the `config` level:
>
> ```
> app.debug = True
> ```
>
> Alternatively, we can use this line of code:
>
> ```
> app.run(debug=True)
> ```
>
> Enabling the debug mode will make the server reload itself in the case of any code changes, and it also provides the very helpful `Werkzeug` debugger when something goes wrong.

There are a bunch of configuration values provided by Flask. We will come across them in the relevant recipes.

As the application grows larger, there originates a need to manage the application's configuration in a separate file as shown here. Being specific to machine-based setups in most cases will most probably not be a part of the version-control system. For this, Flask provides us with multiple ways to fetch configurations. The most frequently used ones are discussed here:

- From a Python configuration file (`*.cfg`), the configuration can be fetched using:

```
app.config.from_pyfile('myconfig.cfg')
```

▸ From an object, the configuration can be fetched using:

```
app.config.from_object('myapplication.default_settings')
```

Alternatively, we can also use:

```
app.config.from_object(__name__) #To load from same file
```

▸ From the environment variable, the configuration can be fetched using:

```
app.config.from_envvar('PATH_TO_CONFIG_FILE')
```

How it works...

Flask is intelligent enough to pick up only those configuration variables that are written in uppercase. This allows us to define any local variables in our configuration files/objects and leave the rest to Flask.

The best practice to use configurations is to have a bunch of default settings in `app.py` or via any object in our application itself and then override the same by loading it from the configuration file. So, the code will look like this:

```
app = Flask(__name__)
DEBUG = True
TESTING = True
app.config.from_object(__name__)
app.config.from_pyfile('/path/to/config/file')
```

Class-based settings

An interesting way of laying out configurations for different deployment modes, such as production, testing, staging, and so on, can be cleanly done using the inheritance pattern of classes. As the project gets bigger, you can have different deployment modes such as development, staging, production, and so on, where each mode can have several different configuration settings, and some settings will remain the same.

How to do it...

We can have a default setting base class, and other classes can inherit this base class and override or add deployment-specific configuration variables.

The following is an example of our default setting base class:

```
class BaseConfig(object):
    'Base config class'
    SECRET_KEY = 'A random secret key'
    DEBUG = True
    TESTING = False
    NEW_CONFIG_VARIABLE = 'my value'

class ProductionConfig(BaseConfig):
    'Production specific config'
    DEBUG = False
    SECRET_KEY = open('/path/to/secret/file').read()

class StagingConfig(BaseConfig):
    'Staging specific config'
    DEBUG = True

class DevelopmentConfig(BaseConfig):
    'Development environment specific config'
    DEBUG = True
    TESTING = True
    SECRET_KEY = 'Another random secret key'
```

 The secret key is stored in a separate file because, for security concerns, it should not be a part of your version-control system. This should be kept in the local filesystem on the machine itself, whether it is your personal machine or a server.

How it works...

Now, we can use any of the preceding classes while loading the application's configuration via `from_object()`. Let's say that we save the preceding class-based configuration in a file named `configuration.py`:

```
app.config.from_object('configuration.DevelopmentConfig')
```

So, overall, this makes the management of configurations for different deployment environments flexible and easier.

Downloading the example code

You can download the example code files for all Packt books you have purchased from your account at `http://www.packtpub.com`. If you purchased this book elsewhere, you can visit `http://www.packtpub.com/support` and register to have the files e-mailed directly to you.

Organization of static files

Organizing static files such as JavaScript, stylesheets, images, and so on efficiently is always a matter of concern for all web frameworks.

How to do it...

Flask recommends a specific way to organize static files in our application:

```
my_app/
    - app.py
    - config.py
    - __init__.py
    - static/
        - css/
        - js/
        - images/
            - logo.png
```

While rendering them in templates (say, the `logo.png` file), we can refer to the static files using the following line of code:

```
<img src='/static/images/logo.png'>
```

How it works...

If there exists a folder named `static` at the application's root level, that is, at the same level as `app.py`, then Flask will automatically read the contents of the folder without any extra configuration.

There's more...

Alternatively, we can provide a parameter named `static_folder` to the application object while defining the application in `app.py`:

```
app = Flask(__name__, static_folder='/path/to/static/folder')
```

In the `img src` path in the *How to do it...* section, `static` refers to the value of `static_url_path` on the application object. This can be modified as follows:

```
app = Flask(
    __name__, static_url_path='/differentstatic',
    static_folder='/path/to/static/folder'
)
```

Now, to render the static file, we will use the following:

```
<img src='/differentstatic/logo.png'>
```

> It is always a good practice to use `url_for` to create the URLs for static files rather than explicitly define them:
> ```
> <img src='{{ url_for('static', filename="logo.png") }}'>
> ```
> We will see more of this in the upcoming chapters.

Being deployment specific with instance folders

Flask provides yet another way of configuration where we can efficiently manage deployment-specific parts. Instance folders allow us to segregate deployment-specific files from our version-controlled application. We know that configuration files can be separate for different deployment environments such as development and production, but there are many more files such as database files, session files, cache files, and other runtime files. So, we can say that an instance folder is like a holder bin for these kinds of files.

How to do it...

By default, the instance folder is picked up from the application automatically if we have a folder named `instance` in our application at the application level:

```
my_app/
    - app.py
    - instance/
        - config.cfg
```

We can also explicitly define the absolute path of the instance folder using the `instance_path` parameter on our application object:

```
app = Flask(
    __name__, instance_path='/absolute/path/to/instance/folder'
)
```

To load the configuration file from the instance folder, we will use the `instance_relative_config` parameter on the application object:

```
app = Flask(__name__, instance_relative_config=True)
```

This tells the application to load the configuration file from the instance folder. The following example shows how this will work:

```
app = Flask(
    __name__, instance_path='path/to/instance/folder',
    instance_relative_config=True
)
app.config.from_pyfile('config.cfg', silent=True)
```

How it works...

In the preceding code, first, the instance folder is loaded from the given path, and then, the configuration file is loaded from the file named `config.cfg` in the given instance folder. Here, `silent=True` is optional and used to suppress the error in case `config.cfg` is not found in the instance folder. If `silent=True` is not given and the file is not found, then the application will fail, giving the following error:

```
IOError: [Errno 2] Unable to load configuration file (No such file or
    directory): '/absolute/path/to/config/file'
```

 It might seem that loading the configuration from the instance folder using `instance_relative_config` is redundant work and can be moved to one of the configuration methods. However, the beauty of this process lies in the fact that the instance folder concept is completely independent of configuration, and `instance_relative_config` just compliments the configuration object.

Composition of views and models

As we go big, we might want to structure our application in a modular manner. We will do this by restructuring our Hello World application.

How to do it...

1. First, create a new folder in our application and move all our files inside this new folder.

2. Then, create `__init__.py` in our folders, which are to be used as modules.

3. After that, create a new file called `run.py` in the topmost folder. As the name implies, this file will be used to run the application.

4. Finally, create separate folders to act as modules.

Refer to the following file structure for a better understanding:

```
flask_app/
    - run.py
    - my_app/
        - __init__.py
        - hello/
            - __init__.py
            - models.py
            - views.py
```

First, the `flask_app/run.py` file will look something like the following lines of code:

```
from my_app import app
app.run(debug=True)
```

Then, the `flask_app/my_app/__init__.py` file will look something like the following lines of code:

```
from flask import Flask
app = Flask(__name__)

import my_app.hello.views
```

Then, we will have an empty file just to make the enclosing folder a Python package, `flask_app/my_app/hello/__init__.py`:

```
# No content.
# We need this file just to make this folder a python module.
```

The models file, `flask_app/my_app/hello/models.py`, has a non-persistent key-value store:

```
MESSAGES = {
    'default': 'Hello to the World of Flask!',
}
```

Finally, the following is the views file, `flask_app/my_app/hello/views.py`. Here, we fetch the message corresponding to the key that is asked for and also have a provision to create or update a message:

```
from my_app import app
from my_app.hello.models import MESSAGES

@app.route('/')
@app.route('/hello')
def hello_world():
```

```
        return MESSAGES['default']


@app.route('/show/<key>')
def get_message(key):
    return MESSAGES.get(key) or "%s not found!" % key


@app.route('/add/<key>/<message>')
def add_or_update_message(key, message):
    MESSAGES[key] = message
    return "%s Added/Updated" % key
```

 Remember that the preceding code is nowhere near production-ready. It is just for demonstration and to make things understandable for new users of Flask.

How it works...

We can see that we have a circular import between `my_app/__init__.py` and `my_app/hello/views.py`, where, in the former, we import `views` from the latter, and in the latter, we import the `app` from the former. So, this actually makes the two modules depend on each other, but here, it is actually fine as we won't be using `views` in `my_app/__init__.py`. We do the import of `views` at the bottom of the file so that they are not used anyway.

We have used a very simple non-persistent in-memory key-value store for the demonstration of the model layout structure. It is true that we could have written the dictionary for the `MESSAGES` hash map in `views.py` itself, but it's best practice to keep the model and view layers separate.

So, we can run this app using just `run.py`:

```
$ python run.py
* Running on http://127.0.0.1:5000/
* Restarting with reloader
```

 The reloader indicates that the application is being run in the debug mode, and the application will reload whenever a change is made in the code.

Now, we can see that we have already defined a default message in MESSAGES. We can view this message by opening `http://127.0.0.1:5000/show/default`. To add a new message, we can type `http://127.0.0.1:5000/add/great/Flask%20is%20 greatgreat!!`. This will update the MESSAGES key-value store to look like the following:

```
MESSAGES = {
    'default': 'Hello to the World of Flask!',
    'great': 'Flask is great!!',
}
```

Now, if we open the link `http://127.0.0.1:5000/show/great` in a browser, we will see our message, which, otherwise, would have appeared as a not-found message.

See also

> ▸ The next recipe, *Creating a modular web app with blueprints*, provides a much better way of organizing your Flask applications and is a readymade solution to circular imports.

Creating a modular web app with blueprints

A **blueprint** is a concept in Flask that helps make large applications really modular. They keep application dispatching simple by providing a central place to register all the components in the application. A blueprint looks like an application object but is not an application. It looks like a pluggable application or a smaller part of a bigger application, but it is not so. A blueprint is actually a set of operations that can be registered on an application and represents how to construct or build an application.

Getting ready

We will take the application from the previous recipe, *Composition of views and models*, as a reference and modify it to work using blueprints.

How to do it...

The following is an example of a simple Hello World application using blueprints. It will work in a manner similar to the previous recipe but is much more modular and extensible.

First, we will start with the `flask_app/my_app/__init__.py` file:

```python
from flask import Flask
from my_app.hello.views import hello

app = Flask(__name__)
app.register_blueprint(hello)
```

Next, the views file, `my_app/hello/views.py`, will look like the following lines of code:

```
from flask import Blueprint
from my_app.hello.models import MESSAGES

hello = Blueprint('hello', __name__)


@hello.route('/')
@hello.route('/hello')
def hello_world():
    return MESSAGES['default']


@hello.route('/show/<key>')
def get_message(key):
    return MESSAGES.get(key) or "%s not found!" % key


@hello.route('/add/<key>/<message>')
def add_or_update_message(key, message):
    MESSAGES[key] = message
    return "%s Added/Updated" % key
```

We have defined a blueprint in the `flask_app/my_app/hello/views.py` file. We don't need the application object anymore here, and our complete routing is defined on a blueprint named `hello`. Instead of `@app.route`, we used `@hello.route`. The same blueprint is imported in `flask_app/my_app/__init__.py` and registered on the application object.

We can create any number of blueprints in our application and do most of the activities that we would do with our application, such as providing different template paths or different static paths. We can even have different URL prefixes or subdomains for our blueprints.

How it works...

This application will work in exactly the same way as the last application. The only difference is in the way the code is organized.

See also

▸   The previous recipe, *Composition of views and models,* is useful to get a background on how this recipe is useful.

Making a Flask app installable using setuptools

So, we have a Flask application now, but how do we install it just like any Python package? It is possible that any other application depends on our application or our application is in fact an extension for Flask and would need to be installed in a Python environment so that it can be used by other applications.

How to do it...

Installing a Flask app can be achieved very easily using the `setuptools` library of Python. We will have to create a file called `setup.py` in our application's folder and configure it to run a setup script for our application. It will take care of any dependencies, descriptions, loading test packages, and so on.

The following is an example of a simple `setup.py` script for our Hello World application:

```python
#!/usr/bin/env python
# -*- coding: UTF-8 -*-
import os
from setuptools import setup

setup(
    name = 'my_app',
    version='1.0',
    license='GNU General Public License v3',
    author='Shalabh Aggarwal',
    author_email='contact@shalabhaggarwal.com',
    description='Hello world application for Flask',
    packages=['my_app'],
    platforms='any',
    install_requires=[
        'flask',
    ],
    classifiers=[
        'Development Status :: 4 - Beta',
        'Environment :: Web Environment',
        'Intended Audience :: Developers',
        'License :: OSI Approved :: GNU General Public License v3',
        'Operating System :: OS Independent',
```

```
            'Programming Language :: Python',
            'Topic :: Internet :: WWW/HTTP :: Dynamic Content',
            'Topic :: Software Development :: Libraries :: Python Modules'
        ],
    )
```

How it works...

In the preceding script, most of the configuration is self-explanatory. The classifiers are used when we make this application available on PyPI. These will help other users search the application using these classifiers.

Now, we can just run this file with the `install` keyword as shown here:

```
$ python setup.py install
```

This will install this application along with all its dependencies mentioned in `install_requires`, that is, Flask and all the dependencies of Flask as well. Then, this app can be used just like any Python package in our Python environment.

See also

► The list of valid trove classifiers can be found at `https://pypi.python.org/pypi?%3Aaction=list_classifiers`

2
Templating with Jinja2

This chapter will cover the basics of Jinja2 templating from the perspective of Flask; we will also learn how to make applications with modular and extensible templates.

In this chapter, we will cover the following recipes:

- ► Bootstrap layout
- ► Block composition and layout inheritance
- ► Creating a custom context processor
- ► Creating a custom Jinja2 filter
- ► Creating a custom macro for forms
- ► Advanced date and time formatting

Introduction

In Flask, we can write a complete web application without the need of any third-party templating engine. For example, have a look at the following code; this is a simple Hello World application with a bit of HTML styling included:

```
from flask import Flask
app = Flask(__name__)

@app.route('/')
@app.route('/hello')
@app.route('/hello/<user>')
def hello_world(user=None):
    user = user or 'Shalabh'
    return '''
<html>
```

```
  <head>
    <title>Flask Framework Cookbook</title>

  </head>
    <body>
      <h1>Hello %s!</h1>
      <p>Welcome to the world of Flask!</p>
    </body>
</html>''' % user

if __name__ == '__main__':
    app.run()
```

Is the preceding pattern of writing the application feasible in the case of large applications that involve thousands of lines of HTML, JS, and CSS code? Obviously not!

Here, templating saves us because we can structure our view code by keeping our templates separate. Flask provides default support for Jinja2, although we can use any templating engine as suited. Furthermore, Jinja2 provides many additional features that make our templates very powerful and modular.

Bootstrap layout

Most of the applications in Flask follow a specific pattern to lay out templates. In this recipe, we will talk about the recommended way of structuring the layout of templates in a Flask application.

Getting ready

By default, Flask expects the templates to be placed inside a folder named `templates` at the application root level. If this folder is present, then Flask will automatically read the contents by making the contents of this folder available for use with the `render_template()` method, which we will use extensively throughout this book.

How to do it...

Let's demonstrate this with a small application. This application is very similar to the one we developed in *Chapter 1, Flask Configurations*. The first thing to do is add a new folder named `templates` under `my_app`. The application structure will now look like the following lines of code:

```
flask_app/
    - run.py
```

```
my_app/
    - __init__.py
    - hello/
        - __init__.py
        - views.py
    - templates
```

We need to make some changes to the application. The `hello_world` method in the views file, `my_app/hello/views.py`, will look like the following lines of code:

```python
from flask import render_template, request

@hello.route('/')
@hello.route('/hello')
def hello_world():
    user = request.args.get('user', 'Shalabh')
    return render_template('index.html', user=user)
```

In the preceding method, we look for a URL query argument, `user`. If it is found, we use it, and if not, we use the default argument, `Shalabh`. Then, this value is passed to the context of the template to be rendered, that is, `index.html`, and the resulting template is rendered.

To start with, the `my_app/templates/index.html` template can be simply put as:

```html
<html>
  <head>
    <title>Flask Framework Cookbook</title>
  </head>
  <body>
    <h1>Hello {{ user }}!</h1>
    <p>Welcome to the world of Flask!</p>
  </body>
</html>
```

How it works...

Now, if we open the URL, `http://127.0.0.1:5000/hello`, in a browser, we will see a response, as shown in the following screenshot:

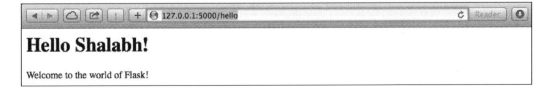

We can also pass a URL argument with the `user` key as `http://127.0.0.1:5000/hello?user=John`; we will see the following response:

Hello John!

Welcome to the world of Flask!

As we can see in `views.py`, the argument passed in the URL is fetched from the `request` object using `request.args.get('user')` and passed to the context of the template being rendered using `render_template`. The argument is then parsed using the Jinja2 placeholder, `{{ user }}`, to fetch the contents from the current value of the `user` variable from the template context. This placeholder evaluates all the expressions that are placed inside it, depending on the template context.

See also

▸   The Jinja2 documentation can be found at `http://jinja.pocoo.org/`. This comes in handy when writing templates.

Block composition and layout inheritance

Usually, any web application will have a number of web pages that will be different from each other. Code blocks such as headers and footers will be the same in almost all the pages throughout the site. Likewise, the menu also remains the same. In fact, usually, just the center container block changes, and the rest usually remains the same. For this, Jinja2 provides a great way of inheritance among templates.

It's a good practice to have a base template where we can structure the basic layout of the site along with the header and footer.

Getting ready

In this recipe, we will try to create a small application where we will have a home page and a product page (such as the ones we see on e-commerce stores). We will use the **Bootstrap** framework to give a minimalistic design to our templates. Bootstrap can be downloaded from `http://getbootstrap.com/`.

Here, we have a hardcoded data store for a few products placed in the `models.py` file. These are read in `views.py` and sent over to the template as template context variables via the `render_template()` method. The rest of the parsing and display is handled by the templating language, which, in our case, is Jinja2.

How to do it...

Have a look at the following layout:

```
flask_app/
    - run.py
    my_app/
        - __init__.py
        - product/
            - __init__.py
            - views.py
            - models.py
        - templates/
            - base.html
            - home.html
            - product.html
        - static/
            - js/
                - bootstrap.min.js
            - css/
                - bootstrap.min.css
                - main.css
```

In the preceding layout, `static/css/bootstrap.min.css` and `static/js/bootstrap.min.js` are standard files and can be downloaded from the Bootstrap website mentioned in the *Getting ready* section. The `run.py` file remains the same as always. The rest of the application is explained here. First, we will define our models, `my_app/product/models.py`. In this chapter, we will work on a simple non-persistent key-value store. We will start with a few hardcoded product records made well in advance:

```
PRODUCTS = {
    'iphone': {
        'name': 'iPhone 5S',
        'category': 'Phones',
        'price': 699,
    },
    'galaxy': {
        'name': 'Samsung Galaxy 5',
        'category': 'Phones',
        'price': 649,
    },
    'ipad-air': {
        'name': 'iPad Air',
        'category': 'Tablets',
        'price': 649,
```

```
        },
    'ipad-mini': {
        'name': 'iPad Mini',
        'category': 'Tablets',
        'price': 549
    }
}
```

Next comes the views, that is, `my_app/product/views.py`. Here, we will follow the blueprint style to write the application:

```
from werkzeug import abort
from flask import render_template
from flask import Blueprint
from my_app.product.models import PRODUCTS

product_blueprint = Blueprint('product', __name__)

@product_blueprint.route('/')
@product_blueprint.route('/home')
def home():
    return render_template('home.html', products=PRODUCTS)

@product_blueprint.route('/product/<key>')
def product(key):
    product = PRODUCTS.get(key)
    if not product:
        abort(404)
    return render_template('product.html', product=product)
```

The name of the blueprint, `product`, that is passed in the `Blueprint` constructor will be appended to the endpoints defined in this blueprint. Have a look at the `base.html` code for clarity.

 The abort() method comes in handy when you want to abort a request with a specific error message. Flask provides basic error message pages that can be customized as needed. We will see them in the *Creating custom 404 and 500 handlers* recipe in *Chapter 4, Working with Views*.

The application's configuration file, my_app/__init__.py, will now look like the following lines of code:

```
from flask import Flask
from my_app.product.views import product_blueprint

app = Flask(__name__)
app.register_blueprint(product_blueprint)
```

Apart from the CSS code provided by Bootstrap, we have a bit of custom CSS code in my_app/static/css/main.css:

```
body {
  padding-top: 50px;
}
.top-pad {
  padding: 40px 15px;
  text-align: center;
}
```

Coming down to templates, the first template acts as the base for all templates. This can aptly be named as base.html and placed at my_app/templates/base.html:

```
<!DOCTYPE html>
<html lang="en">
  <head>
    <meta charset="utf-8">
    <meta http-equiv="X-UA-Compatible" content="IE=edge">
    <meta name="viewport" content="width=device-width, initial-
      scale=1">
    <title>Flask Framework Cookbook</title>
    <link href="{{ url_for('static',
      filename='css/bootstrap.min.css') }}" rel="stylesheet">
    <link href="{{ url_for('static', filename='css/main.css') }}"
      rel="stylesheet">
  </head>
  <body>
    <div class="navbar navbar-inverse navbar-fixed-top"
      role="navigation">
      <div class="container">
        <div class="navbar-header">
          <a class="navbar-brand" href="{{ url_for('product.home')
            }}">Flask Cookbook</a>
        </div>
      </div>
    </div>
```

```html
<div class="container">
  {% block container %}{% endblock %}
</div>

<!-- jQuery (necessary for Bootstrap's JavaScript plugins) -->
<script src="https://ajax.googleapis.com/ajax/libs/jquery/
  2.0.0/jquery.min.js"></script>
<script src="{{ url_for('static', filename='js/
  bootstrap.min.js') }}"></script>
</body>
</html>
```

Most of the preceding code is normal HTML and Jinja2 evaluation placeholders, which were introduced in the previous chapter. An important point to note is how the `url_for()` method is used for blueprint URLs. The blueprint name is appended to all the endpoints. This becomes very useful when we have multiple blueprints inside one application, and some of them can have similar-looking URLs.

In the home page, `my_app/templates/home.html`, we iterate over all the products and show them:

```html
{% extends 'base.html' %}

{% block container %}
  <div class="top-pad">
    {% for id, product in products.iteritems() %}
      <div class="well">
        <h2>
          <a href="{{ url_for('product.product', key=id) }}">{{
            product['name'] }}</a>
          <small>$ {{ product['price'] }}</small>
        </h2>
      </div>
    {% endfor %}
  </div>
{% endblock %}
```

The individual product page, `my_app/templates/product.html`, looks like the following lines of code:

```html
{% extends 'home.html' %}

{% block container %}
  <div class="top-pad">
    <h1>{{ product['name'] }}
      <small>{{ product['category'] }}</small>
```

```
        </h1>
        <h3>$ {{ product['price'] }}</h3>
    </div>
  {% endblock %}
```

How it works...

In the preceding template structure, we saw that there is an inheritance pattern being followed. The `base.html` file acted as the base template for all other templates. The `home.html` file inherited from `base.html`, and `product.html` inherited from `home.html`. In `product.html`, we also saw that we overwrote the `container` block, which was first populated in `home.html`. On running this app, we will see the output as shown in the following screenshots:

The preceding screenshot shows how the home page will look. Note the URL in the browser. This is how the product page will look:

 ▶ Check out the *Creating a custom context processor* and *Creating a custom Jinja2 filter* recipes, which extend this application

Creating a custom context processor

Sometimes, we might want to calculate or process a value directly in the templates. Jinja2 maintains a notion that the processing of logic should be handled in views and not in templates, and thus, it keeps the templates clean. A context processor becomes a handy tool in this case. We can pass our values to a method; this will then be processed in a Python method, and our resultant value will be returned. Therefore, we are essentially just adding a function to the template context (thanks to Python for allowing us to pass around functions just like any other object).

How to do it...

Let's say we want to show the descriptive name of the product in the format `Category / Product-name`:

```
@product_blueprint.context_processor:
def some_processor():
    def full_name(product):
        return '{0} / {1}'.format(product['category'],
            product['name'])
    return {'full_name': full_name}
```

A context is simply a dictionary that can be modified to add or remove values. Any method decorated with `@product_blueprint.context_processor` should return a dictionary that updates the actual context.

We can use the preceding context processor as follows:

```
{{ full_name(product) }}
```

We can add this to our app for the product listing (in the `flask_app/my_app/templates/product.html` file) in the following manner:

```
{% extends 'home.html' %}

{% block container %}
  <div class="top-pad">
    <h4>{{ full_name(product) }}</h4>
    <h1>{{ product['name'] }}
```

```
      <small>{{ product['category'] }}</small>
    </h1>
    <h3>$ {{ product['price'] }}</h3>
  </div>
{% endblock %}
```

The resulting parsed HTML page will look like the following screenshot:

▶ Have a look at the *Block composition and layout inheritance* recipe to understand the context of this recipe

Creating a custom Jinja2 filter

After looking at the previous recipe, experienced developers might think that it was stupid to use a context processor to create a descriptive product name. We can simply write a filter to get the same result; this will make things much cleaner. A filter can be written to display the descriptive name of the product as shown here:

```
@product_blueprint.template_filter('full_name')
def full_name_filter(product):
    return '{0} / {1}'.format(product['category'],
        product['name'])
```

This can be used as follows:

```
{{ product|full_name }}
```

The preceding code will yield a similar result as it did in the previous recipe.

How to do it...

To take things to a higher level, let's create a filter to format the currency based on the current local language:

```
import ccy
from flask import request

@app.template_filter('format_currency')
def format_currency_filter(amount):
    currency_code = ccy.countryccy(request.accept_languages.best[-
    2:])
    return '{0} {1}'.format(currency_code, amount)
```

 The `request.accept_languages` list might now work in cases where a request does not have the `ACCEPT-LANGUAGES` header.

The preceding snippet will require the installation of a new package, `ccy`:

```
$ pip install ccy
```

The filter created here takes the language that best matches the current browser locale (which, in my case, is **en-US**), takes the last two characters from the locale string, and then gets the currency as per the ISO country code that is represented by the last two characters.

How it works...

The filter can be used in our template for the product as shown:

```
<h3>{{ product['price']|format_currency }}</h3>
```

It will yield the result shown in the following screenshot:

▶ Check out the *Block composition and layout inheritance* recipe to understand the context of this recipe

Creating a custom macro for forms

Macros allow us to write reusable pieces of HTML blocks. They are analogous to functions in regular programming languages. We can pass arguments to macros like we do to functions in Python and then use them to process the HTML block. Macros can be called any number of times, and the output will vary as per the logic inside them.

Getting ready

Working with macros in Jinja2 is a very common topic and has a lot of use cases. Here, we will just see how a macro can be created and then used after importing.

How to do it...

One of the most redundant pieces of code in HTML is defining input fields in forms. Most of the fields have similar code with some modifications of style and so on. The following is a macro that creates input fields when called. The best practice is to create the macro in a separate file for better reuseability, for example, `_helpers.html`:

```
{% macro render_field(name, class='', value='', type='text') -%}
    <input type="{{ type }}" name="{{ name }}" class="{{ class }}"
        value="{{ value }}"/>
{%- endmacro %}
```

> The minus sign (-) before/after % will strip the whitespaces after and before these blocks and make the HTML code cleaner to read.

Now, this macro should be imported in the file to be used:

```
{% from '_helpers.jinja' import render_field %}
```

Then, it can simply be called using the following:

```
<fieldset>
    {{ render_field('username', 'icon-user') }}
    {{ render_field('password', 'icon-key', type='password') }}
</fieldset>
```

It is always a good practice to define macros in a different file so as to keep the code clean and increase code readability. If a private macro that cannot be accessed out of the current file is needed, then name the macro with an underscore preceding the name.

Advanced date and time formatting

Date and time formatting is a painful thing to handle in web applications. Handling them at the level of Python, using the `datetime` library increases the overhead and is pretty complex when it comes to handling time zones correctly. We should standardize the timestamps to UTC when stored in the database, but then, the timestamps need to be processed every time they need to be presented to the users worldwide.

It is a smart thing to defer this processing to the client side, that is, the browser. The browser always knows the current time zone of the user and will be able to do the date and time manipulation correctly. Also, this takes off the necessary overhead from our application servers. We will use **Moment.js** for this purpose.

Getting ready

Just like any JS library, Moment.js can be included in our app in the following manner. We will just have to place the JS file, `moment.min.js`, in the `static/js` folder. This can then be used in our HTML file by adding the following statement along with other JS libraries:

```
<script src="/static/js/moment.min.js"></script>
```

The basic usage of Moment.js is shown in the following code. This can be done in the browser console for JavaScript:

```
>>> moment().calendar();
"Today at 4:49 PM"
>>> moment().endOf('day').fromNow();
"in 7 hours"
>>> moment().format('LLLL');
"Tuesday, April 15 2014 4:55 PM"
```

How to do it...

To use Moment.js in our application, the best way will be to write a wrapper in Python and use it via `jinja2` environment variables. Refer to `http://runnable.com/UqGXnKwTGpQgAAO7/dates-and-times-in-flask-for-python` for more information:

```
from jinja2 import Markup

class momentjs(object):
    def __init__(self, timestamp):
```

```
        self.timestamp = timestamp

    # Wrapper to call moment.js method
    def render(self, format):
        return Markup("<script>\ndocument.write(moment(\"%s\").%s)
            ;\n</script>" % (self.timestamp.strftime("%Y-%m-
            %dT%H:%M:%S"), format))

    # Format time
    def format(self, fmt):
        return self.render("format(\"%s\")" % fmt)

    def calendar(self):
        return self.render("calendar()")

    def fromNow(self):
        return self.render("fromNow()")
```

We can add as many Moment.js methods as we want to parse to the preceding class as and when needed. Now, in our `app.py` file, we can set this created class to the `jinja` environment variables:

```
# Set jinja template global
app.jinja_env.globals['momentjs'] = momentjs
```

We can use it in templates as follows:

```
<p>Current time: {{ momentjs(timestamp).calendar() }}</p>
<br/>
<p>Time: {{momentjs(timestamp).format('YYYY-MM-DD HH:mm:ss')}}</p>
<br/>
<p>From now: {{momentjs(timestamp).fromNow()}}</p>
```

See more

▶ Read more about the Moment.js library at `http://momentjs.com/`

3

Data Modeling in Flask

This chapter covers one of the most important parts of any application, that is, the interaction with database systems. This chapter will take us through how Flask can connect to database systems, define models, and query the databases for retrieval and feeding of data.

In this chapter, we will cover the following recipes:

- ▶ Creating a SQLAlchemy DB instance
- ▶ Creating a basic product model
- ▶ Creating a relational category model
- ▶ Database migration using Alembic and Flask-Migrate
- ▶ Model data indexing with Redis
- ▶ Opting the NoSQL way with MongoDB

Introduction

Flask has been designed to be flexible enough to support any database. The simplest way would be to use the direct sqlite3 package, which is a DB-API 2.0 interface and does not actually give an ORM. Here, we will use SQL queries to talk with the database. This approach is not suggested for large projects as it can eventually become a nightmare to maintain the application. Also, with this approach, the models are virtually non-existent and everything happens in the view functions, where we write queries to interact with the DB.

In this chapter, we will talk about creating an ORM layer for our Flask applications with SQLAlchemy for relational database systems, which is recommended and widely used for applications of any size. Also, we will have a glance over how to write a Flask app with the NoSQL database system.

ORM refers to Object Relational Mapping/Modeling and implies how our application's data models store and deal with data at a conceptual level. A powerful ORM makes designing and querying business logic easy and streamlined.

Creating a SQLAlchemy DB instance

SQLAlchemy is a Python SQL toolkit and provides an ORM that gives the flexibility and power of SQL with the feel of Python's object-oriented nature.

Getting ready

Flask-SQLAlchemy is the extension that provides the SQLAlchemy interface for Flask.

This extension can be simply installed using `pip` as follows:

```
$ pip install flask-sqlalchemy
```

The first thing to keep in mind with Flask-SQLAlchemy is the application config parameter that tells SQLAlchemy about the location of the database to be used:

```
app.config['SQLALCHEMY_DATABASE_URI'] = os.environ('DATABASE_URI')
```

This `SQLALCHEMY_DATABASE_URI` is a combination of the database protocol, any authentication needed, and also the name of the database. In the case of SQLite, this would look something like the following:

```
sqlite:////tmp/test.db
```

In the case of PostgreSQL, it would look like the following:

```
postgresql://yourusername:yourpassword@localhost/yournewdb.
```

This extension then provides a class named `Model` that helps in defining models for our application. Read more about database URLs at `http://docs.sqlalchemy.org/en/rel_0_9/core/engines.html#database-urls`.

For all database systems other than SQLite, separate libraries are needed. For example, for using PostgreSQL, you would need **psycopg2**.

How to do it...

Let's demonstrate this with a small application. We will build over this application in the next few recipes. Here, we will just see how to create a db instance and some basic DB commands. The file's structure would look as follows:

```
flask_catalog/
    - run.py
    my_app/
        - __init__.py
```

First, we start with `flask_app/run.py`. It is the usual run file that we have read about up to now in this book:

```
from my_app import app
app.run(debug=True)
```

Then we configure our application configuration file, that is, `flask_app/my_app/__init__.py`.

```
from flask import Flask
from flask.ext.sqlalchemy import SQLAlchemy

app = Flask(__name__)
app.config['SQLALCHEMY_DATABASE_URI'] = 'sqlite:////tmp/test.db'
db = SQLAlchemy(app)
```

Here, we configure our application to point `SQLALCHEMY_DATABASE_URI` to a specific location. Then, we create an object of `SQLAlchemy` with the name db. As the name suggests, this is the object that will handle all our ORM-related activities. As mentioned earlier, this object has a class named `Model`, which provides the base for creating models in Flask. Any class can just subclass or inherit the `Model` class to create models, which will act as database tables.

Now, if we open the URL `http://127.0.0.1:5000` in a browser, we will actually see nothing. This is because there is nothing in the application.

There's more...

Sometimes, you might want a single SQLAlchemy db instance to be used across multiple applications or create an application dynamically. In such cases, we might not prefer to bind our db instance to a single application. Here, we will have to work with application contexts to achieve the desired outcome.

In this case, we will register our application with SQLAlchemy differently, as follows:

```
from flask import Flask
from flask.ext.sqlalchemy import SQLAlchemy

db = SQLAlchemy()

def create_app():
    app = Flask(__name__)
    db.init_app(app)
    return app
```

 The preceding approach can be taken up while initializing the app with any Flask extension and is very common when dealing with real-life applications.

Now, all the operations that were earlier possible globally with the db instance will now require a Flask application context at all times:

```
Flask application context
>>> from my_app import create_app
>>> app = create_app()
>>> app.test_request_context().push()
>>> # Do whatever needs to be done
>>> app.test_request_context().pop()
Or we can use context manager
with app():
    # We have flask application context now till we are inside the
with block
```

See also

▶ The next couple of recipes will extend the current application to make a complete application, which will help us understand the ORM layer better

Creating a basic product model

In this recipe, we will create an application that will help us store products to be displayed on the catalog section of a website. It should be possible to add products to the catalog and delete them as and when required. As we saw in previous chapters, this is possible to do using non-persistent storage as well. But, here we will store data in a database to have persistent storage.

How to do it...

The new directory layout will look as follows:

```
flask_catalog/
    - run.py
    my_app/
        - __init__.py
        catalog/
            - __init__.py
            - views.py
            - models.py
```

First of all, we will start by modifying our application configuration file, that is, `flask_catalog/my_app/__init__.py`:

```python
from flask import Flask
from flask.ext.sqlalchemy import SQLAlchemy

app = Flask(__name__)
app.config['SQLALCHEMY_DATABASE_URI'] = 'sqlite:////tmp/test.db'
db = SQLAlchemy(app)

from my_app.catalog.views import catalog
app.register_blueprint(catalog)

db.create_all()
```

The last statement in the file is `db.create_all()`, which tells the application to create all the tables in the database specified. So, as soon as the application runs, all the tables will be created if they are not already there. Now is the time to create models that are placed in `flask_catalog/my_app/catalog/models.py`:

```python
from my_app import db

class Product(db.Model):
    id = db.Column(db.Integer, primary_key=True)
    name = db.Column(db.String(255))
    price = db.Column(db.Float)

    def __init__(self, name, price):
        self.name = name
        self.price = price

    def __repr__(self):
        return '<Product %d>' % self.id
```

In this file, we have created a model named `Product` that has three fields, namely `id`, `name`, and `price`. The `id` field is a self-generated field in the database that will store the ID of the record and is the primary key. `name` is a field of type string and `price` is of type float.

Now, we add a new file for views, which is `flask_catalog/my_app/catalog/views.py`. In this file, we have multiple view methods that control how we deal with the product model and the web application in general:

```python
from flask import request, jsonify, Blueprint
from my_app import app, db
from my_app.catalog.models import Product

catalog = Blueprint('catalog', __name__)

@catalog.route('/')
@catalog.route('/home')
def home():
    return "Welcome to the Catalog Home."
```

This method handles how the home page or the application landing page looks or responds to the users. You would most probably use a template for rendering this in your applications. We will cover this a bit later. Have a look at the following code:

```python
@catalog.route('/product/<id>')
def product(id):
    product = Product.query.get_or_404(id)
    return 'Product - %s, $%s' % (product.name, product.price)
```

This method controls the output to be shown when a user looks up a specific product using its ID. We filter for the product using the ID and then return its information if the product is found; if not, we abort with a 404 error. Consider the following code:

```python
@catalog.route('/products')
def products():
    products = Product.query.all()
    res = {}
    for product in products:
        res[product.id] = {
            'name': product.name,
            'price': str(product.price)
        }
    return jsonify(res)
```

This method returns the list of all products in the database in JSON format. Consider the following code:

```
@catalog.route('/product-create', methods=['POST',])
def create_product():
    name = request.form.get('name')
    price = request.form.get('price')
    product = Product(name, price)
    db.session.add(product)
    db.session.commit()
    return 'Product created.'
```

This method controls the creation of a product in the database. We first get the information from a request and then create a `Product` instance from this information. Then, we add this `Product` instance to the database session and finally commit to save the record to the database.

How it works...

In the beginning, the database is empty and has no product. This can be confirmed by opening `http://127.0.0.1:5000/products` in a browser. This would result in an empty page with just **{}**.

Now, first we would want to create a product. For this, we need to send a POST request, which can be sent from the Python prompt using the `requests` library easily:

```
>>> import requests
>>> requests.post('http://127.0.0.1:5000/product-create',
    data={'name': 'iPhone 5S', 'price': '549.0'})
```

To confirm whether the product is in the database now, we can open `http://127.0.0.1:5000/products` in the browser again. This time, it would show a JSON dump of the product details.

See also

▶ The next recipe, *Creating a relational category model*, demonstrates the relational aspect of tables

Creating a relational category model

In our previous recipe, we created a simple product model that had a couple of fields. However, in practice, applications are much more complex and have various relationships among their tables. These relationships can be one-to-one, one-to-many, many-to-one, or many-to-many. We will try to understand some of them in this recipe with the help of an example.

How to do it...

Let's say we want to have product categories where each category can have multiple products, but each product should have at least one category. Let's do this by modifying some files from the preceding application. We will make modifications to both models and views. In models, we will add a Category model, and in views, we will add new methods to handle category-related calls and also modify the existing methods to accommodate the newly added feature.

First, we will modify our models.py file to add the Category model and some modifications to the Product model:

```python
from my_app import db

class Product(db.Model):
    id = db.Column(db.Integer, primary_key=True)
    name = db.Column(db.String(255))
    price = db.Column(db.Float)
    category_id = db.Column(db.Integer,
      db.ForeignKey('category.id'))
    category = db.relationship(
        'Category', backref=db.backref('products', lazy='dynamic')
    )

    def __init__(self, name, price, category):
        self.name = name
        self.price = price
        self.category = category

    def __repr__(self):
        return '<Product %d>' % self.id
```

In the preceding `Product` model, notice the newly added fields for `category_id` and `category`. The `category_id` field is the foreign key to the `Category` model, and `category` represents the relationship table. As evident from the definitions themselves, one of them is a relationship, and the other uses this relationship to store the foreign key value in the database. This is a simple many-to-one relationship from product to category. Also, notice the `backref` argument in the `category` field; this argument allows us to access products from the `Category` model by writing something as simple as `category.products` in our views. This acts like the one-to-many relationship from the other end. Consider the following code:

```
class Category(db.Model):
    id = db.Column(db.Integer, primary_key=True)
    name = db.Column(db.String(100))

    def __init__(self, name):
        self.name = name

    def __repr__(self):
        return '<Category %d>' % self.id
```

The preceding code is the `Category` model, which has just one field called `name`.

Now, we will modify our `views.py` file to accommodate the changes in our models:

```
from my_app.catalog.models import Product, Category

@catalog.route('/products')
def products():
    products = Product.query.all()
    res = {}
    for product in products:
        res[product.id] = {
            'name': product.name,
            'price': product.price,
            'category': product.category.name
        }
    return jsonify(res)
```

Here, we have just one change where we are sending the category name and the product's JSON data is being generated to be returned. Consider the following code:

```
@catalog.route('/product-create', methods=['POST',])
def create_product():
    name = request.form.get('name')
    price = request.form.get('price')
    categ_name = request.form.get('category')
    category = Category.query.filter_by(name=categ_name).first()
    if not category:
        category = Category(categ_name)
    product = Product(name, price, category)
    db.session.add(product)
    db.session.commit()
    return 'Product created.'
```

Check out how we are looking for the category before creating the product. We will first search for an existing category with the category name in the request. If an existing category is found, we will use it for product creation; otherwise, we will create a new category. Consider the following code:

```
@catalog.route('/category-create', methods=['POST',])
def create_category():
    name = request.form.get('name')
    category = Category(name)
    db.session.add(category)
    db.session.commit()
    return 'Category created.'
```

The preceding code is a relatively simple method for creating a category using the name provided in the request. Consider the following code:

```
@catalog.route('/categories')
def categories():
    categories = Category.query.all()
    res = {}
    for category in categories:
        res[category.id] = {
            'name': category.name
        }
        for product in category.products:
            res[category.id]['products'] = {
                'id': product.id,
                'name': product.name,
                'price': product.price
            }
    return jsonify(res)
```

The preceding method does a bit of tricky stuff. Here, we fetched all the categories from the database, and then for each category, we fetched all the products and then returned all the data as a JSON dump.

See also

▶ Read through the *Creating a basic product model* recipe to understand the context of this recipe and how this recipe works for a browser

Database migration using Alembic and Flask-Migrate

Now, let's say we want to update our models to have a new field called `company` in our `Product` model. One way is to drop the database and then create a new one using `db.drop_all()` and `db.create_all()`. However, this approach cannot be followed for applications in production or even in staging. We would want to migrate our database to match the newly updated model with all the data intact.

For this, we have **Alembic**, which is a Python-based tool to manage database migrations and uses SQLAlchemy as the underlying engine. Alembic provides automatic migrations to a great extent with some limitations (of course, we cannot expect any tool to be seamless). To act as the icing on the cake, we have a Flask extension called **Flask-Migrate**, which eases the process of migrations even more.

Getting ready

First of all, we will install Flask-Migrate:

```
$ pip install Flask-Migrate
```

This will also install Flask-Script and Alembic, among some other dependencies. Flask-Script powers Flask-Migrate to provide some easy-to-use command-line arguments, which provide a good level of abstraction to the users and hide all the complex stuff (which are actually not very difficult to customize if needed).

How to do it...

To enable migrations, we will need to modify our app definition a bit.

The following code shows what such a config looks like if we modify the code for our catalog application.

The following lines of code show how `my_app/__init__.py` looks:

```python
from flask import Flask
from flask.ext.sqlalchemy import SQLAlchemy
from flask.ext.script import Manager
from flask.ext.migrate import Migrate, MigrateCommand

app = Flask(__name__)
app.config['SQLALCHEMY_DATABASE_URI'] = 'sqlite:////tmp/test.db'
db = SQLAlchemy(app)
migrate = Migrate(app, db)

manager = Manager(app)
manager.add_command('db', MigrateCommand)

import my_app.catalog.views

db.create_all()
```

Also, we will have to make a small change in `run.py`:

```python
from my_app import manager
manager.run()
```

This change in `run.py` is because now we are using the Flask script manager to handle the running of our application. The script manager also provides extra command-line arguments as specified. In this example, we will have `db` as a command-line argument.

If we pass `--help` to `run.py` while running it as a script, the terminal will show all the available options, as shown in the following screenshot:

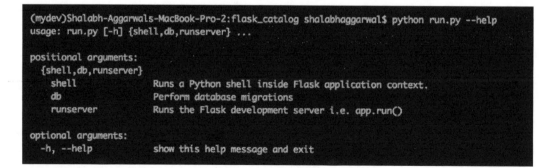

```
(mydev)Shalabh-Aggarwals-MacBook-Pro-2:flask_catalog shalabhaggarwal$ python run.py --help
usage: run.py [-h] {shell,db,runserver} ...

positional arguments:
  {shell,db,runserver}
    shell              Runs a Python shell inside Flask application context.
    db                 Perform database migrations
    runserver          Runs the Flask development server i.e. app.run()

optional arguments:
  -h, --help           show this help message and exit
```

Now, to run the application, we will have to run the following:

```
$ python run.py runserver
```

To initialize migrations, we have to run the `init` command:

```
$ python run.py db init
```

After we make changes to models, we have to call the `migrate` command:

```
$ python run.py db migrate
```

To make the changes reflect on the database, we will call the `upgrade` command:

```
$ python run.py db upgrade
```

How it works...

Now, let's say we modify the model of our `product` table to add a new field called `company` as shown here:

```
class Product(db.Model):
    # ...
    # Same product model as last recipe
    # ...
    company = db.Column(db.String(100))
```

The result of `migrate` will be something like the following snippet:

```
$ python run.py db migrate

INFO   [alembic.migration] Context impl SQLiteImpl.

INFO   [alembic.migration] Will assume non-transactional DDL.

INFO   [alembic.autogenerate.compare] Detected added column
    'product.company'   Generating <path/to/application>/
    flask_catalog/migrations/versions/2c08f71f9253_.py ... done
```

In the preceding code, we can see that Alembic compares the new model with the database table and detects a newly added column for `company` in the `product` table (created by the `Product` model).

Similarly, the output of `upgrade` will be something like the following snippet:

```
$ python run.py db upgrade

INFO   [alembic.migration] Context impl SQLiteImpl.

INFO   [alembic.migration] Will assume non-transactional DDL.

INFO   [alembic.migration] Running upgrade None -> 2c08f71f9253, empty
    message
```

Here, Alembic performs the upgrade of the database for the migration detected earlier. We can see a hex code in the preceding output. This represents the revision of the migration performed. This is for internal use by Alembic to track the changes to database tables.

See also

▶ Check out the *Creating a basic product model* recipe to understand the context of this recipe

Model data indexing with Redis

There might be some features that we want to implement but do not want to have a persistent storage for them. So, we would like to have these stored in a cache-like storage for a short period of time and then hide them, for example, showing a list of the recently visited products to the visitors on the website.

Getting ready

We will do this with the help of **Redis**, which can be installed using the following command:

```
$ pip install redis
```

Make sure that you run the Redis server for the connection to happen. To install and run a Redis server, refer to `http://redis.io/topics/quickstart`.

Then, we need to have the connection open to Redis. This can be done by adding the following lines of code to `my_app/__init__.py`:

```
from redis import Redis
redis = Redis()
```

We can do this in our application file, where we will define the app, or in the views file, where we will use it. It is preferred that you do this in the application file because then the connection will be open throughout the application, and the `redis` object can be used by just importing it where needed.

How to do it...

We will maintain a set in Redis that will store the recently visited products. This will be populated whenever we visit a product. The entry will expire after 10 minutes. This change goes in `views.py`:

```
from my_app import redis

@catalog.route('/product/<id>')
def product(id):
    product = Product.query.get_or_404(id)
    product_key = 'product-%s' % product.id
    redis.set(product_key, product.name)
    redis.expire(product_key, 600)
    return 'Product - %s, $%s' % (product.name, product.price)
```

It is a good practice to fetch the `expire` time, that is, `600`, from a configuration value. This can be set on the application object in `my_app/__init__.py`, and then can be fetched from here.

In the preceding method, note the `set()` and `expire()` methods on the `redis` object. First, we set the product ID using the `product_key` value in the Redis store. Then, we set the `expire` time of the key to `600` seconds.

Now, we will look for the keys that are still alive in the cache and then fetch the products corresponding to these keys and return them:

```
@catalog.route('/recent-products')
def recent_products():
    keys_alive = redis.keys('product-*')
    products = [redis.get(k) for k in keys_alive]
    return jsonify({'products': products})
```

How it works...

An entry is added to the store whenever a user visits a product, and the entry is kept there for 600 seconds (10 minutes). Now, this product will be listed in the recent products list for the next 10 minutes unless it is visited again, which will reset the time to 10 minutes again.

Opting the NoSQL way with MongoDB

Sometimes, the data to be used in the application we are building might not be structured at all, can be semi-structured, or can be data whose schema changes over time. In such cases, we would refrain from using an RDBMS, as it adds to the pain and is difficult to understand and maintain. For such cases, we might want to use a **NoSQL** database.

Also, as a result of fast and quick development in the currently prevalent development environment, it is not always possible to design the perfect schema the first time. NoSQL provides the flexibility to modify the schema without much of a hassle.

In production environments, the database usually grows to a huge size in a short period of time. This drastically affects the performance of the overall system. Vertical- and horizontal-scaling techniques are available as well, but they can be very costly at times. In such cases, a NoSQL database can be considered, as it is designed from scratch for similar purposes. The ability of NoSQL databases to run on large multiple clusters and handle huge volumes of data generated with high velocity makes them a good choice when looking to handle scaling issues with traditional RDBMS.

Here, we will use **MongoDB** to understand how to integrate NoSQL with Flask.

Getting ready

There are many extensions available to use Flask with MongoDB. We will use Flask-MongoEngine as it provides a good level of abstraction, which makes it easier to understand. It can be installed using the following command:

```
$ pip install flask-mongoengine
```

Remember to run the MongoDB server for the connection to happen. For more details on installing and running MongoDB, refer to http://docs.mongodb.org/manual/installation/.

How to do it...

The following is an application that is a rewrite of our catalog application using MongoDB. The first change comes to our configuration file, my_app/__init__.py:

```python
from flask import Flask
from flask.ext.mongoengine import MongoEngine
from redis import Redis


app = Flask(__name__)
app.config['MONGODB_SETTINGS'] = {'DB': 'my_catalog'}
app.debug = True
db = MongoEngine(app)

redis = Redis()

from my_app.catalog.views import catalog
app.register_blueprint(catalog)
```

Note that instead of the usual SQLAlchemy-centric settings, we now have MONGODB_SETTINGS. Here, we just specify the name of the database to use. First, we will have to manually create this database in MongoDB using the command line:

```
>>> mongo
MongoDB shell version: 2.6.4
> use my_catalog
switched to db my_catalog
```

Next, we will create a `Product` model using MongoDB fields. This happens as usual in the models file, `flask_catalog/my_app/catalog/models.py`:

```python
import datetime
from my_app import db


class Product(db.Document):
    created_at = db.DateTimeField(
        default=datetime.datetime.now, required=True
    )
    key = db.StringField(max_length=255, required=True)
    name = db.StringField(max_length=255, required=True)
    price = db.DecimalField()

    def __repr__(self):
        return '<Product %r>' % self.id
```

> Note the MongoDB fields used to create the model and their similarity with the SQLAlchemy fields used in the previous recipes. Here, instead of an ID field, we have `created_at`, which stores the timestamp in which the record was created.

The following is the views file, namely `flask_catalog/my_app/catalog/views.py`:

```python
from decimal import Decimal
from flask import request, Blueprint, jsonify
from my_app.catalog.models import Product

catalog = Blueprint('catalog', __name__)

@catalog.route('/')
@catalog.route('/home')
def home():
    return "Welcome to the Catalog Home."

@catalog.route('/product/<key>')
def product(key):
    product = Product.objects.get_or_404(key=key)
    return 'Product - %s, $%s' % (product.name, product.price)

@catalog.route('/products')
def products():
    products = Product.objects.all()
```

```
    res = {}
    for product in products:
        res[product.key] = {
            'name': product.name,
            'price': str(product.price),
        }
    return jsonify(res)

@catalog.route('/product-create', methods=['POST',])
def create_product():
    name = request.form.get('name')
    key = request.form.get('key')
    price = request.form.get('price')
    product = Product(
        name=name,
        key=key,
        price=Decimal(price)
    )
    product.save()
    return 'Product created.'
```

You will notice it is very similar to the views created for the SQLAlchemy-based models. There are just a few differences in the methods that are called from the MongoEngine extension; they should be easy to understand.

See also

▶ Check out the *Creating a basic product model* recipe to understand how this application works

4
Working with Views

For any web application, it is very important to control how you interact with web requests and the proper responses to be catered for these requests. This chapter takes us through the various methods of handling the requests properly and designing them in the best way.

In this chapter, we will cover the following recipes:

- ▶ Writing function-based views and URL routes
- ▶ Class-based views
- ▶ URL routing and product-based pagination
- ▶ Rendering to templates
- ▶ Dealing with XHR requests
- ▶ Decorator to handle requests beautifully
- ▶ Creating custom 404 and 500 handlers
- ▶ Flashing messages for better user feedback
- ▶ SQL-based searching

Introduction

Flask offers several ways of designing and laying out the URL routing for our applications. Also, it gives us the flexibility to keep the architecture of our views as simple as just functions to a more complex but extensible class-based layout (which can be inherited and modified as needed). In earlier versions, Flask just had function-based views. However, later, in version 0.7, inspired by Django, Flask introduced the concept of pluggable views, which allows us to have classes and then write methods in these classes. This also makes the process of building a RESTful API pretty simple. Also, we can always go a level deeper into Werkzeug and use the more flexible but slightly more complex concept of URL maps. In fact, large applications and frameworks prefer using URL maps.

Writing function-based views and URL routes

This is the simplest way of writing views and URL routes in Flask. We can just write a method and decorate it with the endpoint.

Getting ready

To understand this recipe, we can start with any Flask application. The app can be a new, empty, or any complex app. We just need to understand the methods outlined in this recipe.

How to do it...

The following are the three most widely used, different kinds of requests, demonstrated with short examples.

A simple GET request

Consider the following code:

```
@app.route('/a-get-request')
def get_request():
    bar = request.args.get('foo', 'bar')
    return 'A simple Flask request where foo is %s' % bar
```

This is a simple example of what a GET request looks like. Here, we just check whether the URL query has an argument called `foo`. If yes, we display this in the response; otherwise, the default is `bar`.

A simple POST request

Consider the following code:

```
@app.route('/a-post-request', methods=['POST'])
def post_request():
    bar = request.form.get('foo', 'bar')
    return 'A simple Flask request where foo is %s' % bar
```

This is similar to the GET request but with a few differences, that is, the route now contains an extra argument called `methods`. Also, instead of `request.args`, we now use `request.form`, as POST assumes that the data is submitted in a form manner.

Is it really necessary to write GET and POST in separate methods? No!

A simple GET/POST request

Consider the following code:

```
@app.route('/a-request', methods=['GET', 'POST'])
def some_request():
    if request.method == 'GET':
        bar = request.args.get('foo', 'bar')
    else:
        bar = request.form.get('foo', 'bar')
    return 'A simple Flask request where foo is %s' % bar
```

Here, we can see that we have amalgamated the first two methods into one, and now, both GET and POST are handled by one view function.

How it works...

Let's try to understand how the preceding methods work.

By default, any Flask view function supports only GET requests. In order to support or handle any other kind of request, we have to specifically tell our `route()` decorator about the methods we want to support. This is exactly what we did in our last two methods for POST and GET/POST.

For GET requests, the `request` object will look for `args`, that is, `request.args.get()`, and for POST, it will look for `form`, that is, `request.form.get()`.

Also, if we try to make a GET request to a method that supports only POST, the request will fail with a 405 HTTP error. The same holds true for all the methods. See the following screenshot:

`127.0.0.1:5000/a-post-request`

Method Not Allowed

The method is not allowed for the requested URL.

There's more...

Sometimes, we might want to have a URL map kind of a pattern, where we prefer to define all the URL rules with endpoints at a single place rather than them being scattered all around the application. For this, we will need to define our methods without the `route()` decorator and define the route on our application object as shown here:

```
def get_request():

    bar = request.args.get('foo', 'bar')
```

```
           return 'A simple Flask request where foo is %s' % bar

       app = Flask(__name__)
       app.add_url_rule('/a-get-request', view_func=get_request)
```

Make sure that you give the correct relative path to the method assigned to `view_func`.

Class-based views

Flask introduced the concept of pluggable views in version 0.7; this added a lot of flexibility to the existing implementation. We can write views in the form of classes; these views can be written in a generic fashion and allow for an easy and understandable inheritance.

Getting ready

Refer to the previous recipe, *Writing function-based views and URL routes*, to understand the basic function-based views first.

How to do it...

Flask provides a class named `View`, which can be inherited to add our custom behavior.

The following is an example of a simple GET request:

```
       from flask.views import View

       class GetRequest(View):

           def dispatch_request(self):
               bar = request.args.get('foo', 'bar')
               return 'A simple Flask request where foo is %s' % bar

       app.add_url_rule(
           '/a-get-request', view_func=GetRequest.as_view('get_request')
       )
```

To accommodate both the GET and POST requests, we can write the following code:

```
       from flask.views import View

       class GetPostRequest(View):
           methods = ['GET', 'POST']

           def dispatch_request(self):
               if request.method == 'GET':
```

```
        bar = request.args.get('foo', 'bar')
    if request.method == 'POST':
        bar = request.form.get('foo', 'bar')
    return 'A simple Flask request where foo is %s' % bar

app.add_url_rule(
    '/a-request',
    view_func=GetPostRequest.as_view('a_request')
)
```

How it works...

We know that by default, any Flask view function supports only GET requests. The same applies in the case of class-based views. In order to support or handle any other kind of request, we have to specifically tell our class, via a class attribute called `methods`, about the HTTP methods we want to support. This is exactly what we did in our previous example of GET/POST requests.

For GET requests, the `request` object will look for `args`, that is, `request.args.get()`, and for POST, it will look for `form`, that is, `request.form.get()`.

Also, if we try to make a GET request to a method that supports only POST, the request will fail with a 405 HTTP error. The same holds true for all the methods.

There's more...

Now, many of us might be thinking that is it not possible to just declare GET and POST methods inside a `View` class and let Flask handle the rest of the stuff. The answer to this question is `MethodView`. Let's write our previous snippet using `MethodView`:

```
from flask.views import MethodView
class GetPostRequest(MethodView):

    def get(self):
        bar = request.args.get('foo', 'bar')
        return 'A simple Flask request where foo is %s' % bar

    def post(self):
        bar = request.form.get('foo', 'bar')
        return 'A simple Flask request where foo is %s' % bar

app.add_url_rule(
    '/a-request',
    view_func=GetPostRequest.as_view('a_request')
)
```

See also

▶   Refer to the previous recipe, *Writing function-based views and URL routes*,
    to understand the contrast between class- and function-based views

URL routing and product-based pagination

At times, we might have to parse the various parts of a URL in different parts. For example,
our URL can have an integer part, a string part, a string part of specific length, slashes in the
URL, and so on. We can parse all these combinations in our URLs using URL converters. In
this recipe, we will see how to do this. Also, we will learn how to implement pagination using
the Flask-SQLAlchemy extension.

Getting ready

We have already seen several instances of basic URL converters. In this recipe, we will look at
some advanced URL converters and learn how to use them.

How to do it...

Let's say we have a URL route defined as follows:

```
@app.route('/test/<name>')
def get_name(name):
    return name
```

Here, `http://127.0.0.1:5000/test/Shalabh` will result in `Shalabh` being parsed and
passed in the `name` argument of the `get_name` method. This is a unicode or string converter,
which is the default one and need not be specified explicitly.

We can also have strings with specific lengths. Let's say we want to parse a URL that can
contain a country code or currency code. Country codes are usually two characters long
and currency codes are three characters long. This can be done as follows:

```
@app.route('/test/<string(minlength=2,maxlength=3):code>')
def get_name(code):
    return code
```

This will match both US and USD in the URL, that is, `http://127.0.0.1:5000/test/USD`
and `http://127.0.0.1:5000/test/US` will be treated similarly. We can also match the
exact length using the `length` parameter instead of `minlength` and `maxlength`.

We can also parse integer values in a similar fashion:

```
@app.route('/test/<int:age>')
def get_age(age):
    return str(age)
```

We can also specify the minimum and maximum values that can be accepted. For example, we can have `@app.route('/test/<int(min=18,max=99):age>')`. We can also parse float values using `float` in place of `int` in the preceding example.

Sometimes, we might want to escape slashes in our URLs or parse URLs with some filesystem path or another URL's path. This can be done as follows:

```
@app.route('/test/<path:file>/end')
def get_file(file):
    return file
```

This will catch something like `http://127.0.0.1:5000/test/usr/local/app/settings.py/end` and identify `usr/local/app/settings.py` as the file argument to be passed to the method.

Adding pagination to applications

In the *Creating a basic product model* recipe in *Chapter 3, Data Modeling in Flask*, we created a handler to list out all the products in our database. If we have thousands of products, then generating the list of all these products in one go can take a lot of time. Also, if we have to render these products on a template, then we would not want to show more than 10-20 products on a page in one go. Pagination proves to be of great help in building great applications.

Let's modify the `products()` method to list products to support pagination:

```
@catalog.route('/products')
@catalog.route('/products/<int:page>')
def products(page=1):
    products = Product.query.paginate(page, 10).items
    res = {}
    for product in products:
        res[product.id] = {
            'name': product.name,
            'price': product.price,
            'category': product.category.name
        }
    return jsonify(res)
```

In the preceding handler, we added a new URL route that adds a `page` parameter to the URL. Now, `http://127.0.0.1:5000/products` will be the same as `http://127.0.0.1:5000/products/1`, and both will return the list of the first 10 products from the DB. Then, `http://127.0.0.1:5000/products/2` will return the next 10 products and so on.

> The `paginate()` method takes three arguments and returns an object of the `Pagination` class. These three arguments are:
>
> ▶ `page`: This is the current page to be listed.
> ▶ `per_page`: This is the number of items to be listed per page.
> ▶ `error_out`: If no items are found for the page, then this aborts with a 404 error. To prevent this behavior, set this parameter to `False`, and then, it will just return an empty list.

See also

▶ The *Creating a basic product model* recipe in *Chapter 3, Data Modeling in Flask*, to understand the context of this recipe for pagination

Rendering to templates

After writing the views, we will surely want to render the content on a template and get information from the underlying database.

Getting ready

To render to templates, we will use Jinja2 as the templating language. Refer to *Chapter 2, Templating with Jinja2*, to understand templating in depth.

How to do it...

We will again work in reference to our existing catalog application from the previous recipe. We will now modify our views to render templates and then display data from the database in these templates.

The following is the modified `views.py` code and the templates. The complete app can be downloaded from the code bundle provided with this book.

We will start by modifying our views, that is, `flask_catalog_template/my_app/catalog/views.py`, to render templates on specific handlers:

```
from flask import render_template


@catalog.route('/')
@catalog.route('/home')
def home():
    return render_template('home.html')
```

Notice the `render_template()` method. This method will render `home.html` when the `home` handler is called. Consider the following code:

```
@catalog.route('/product/<id>')
def product(id):
    product = Product.query.get_or_404(id)
    return render_template('product.html', product=product)
```

Here, the `product.html` template will be rendered with the `product` object in the template context. Consider the following code:

```
@catalog.route('/products')
@catalog.route('/products/<int:page>')
def products(page=1):
    products = Product.query.paginate(page, 10)
    return render_template('products.html', products=products)
```

Here, the `products.html` template will be rendered with the list of paginated `product` objects in the context. Consider the following code:

```
@catalog.route('/product-create', methods=['POST',])
def create_product():
    # ... Same code as before ...
    return render_template('product.html', product=product)
```

As we can see in the preceding code, in this case, the template corresponding to the newly created product will be rendered. This can also be done using `redirect()`, but we will cover this at a later stage. Have a look at the following code:

```
@catalog.route('/category-create', methods=['POST',])
def create_category():
    # ... Same code as before ...
    return render_template('category.html', category=category)


@catalog.route('/category/<id>')
def category(id):
```

```
        category = Category.query.get_or_404(id)
        return render_template('category.html', category=category)


    @catalog.route('/categories')
    def categories():
        categories = Category.query.all()
        return render_template('categories.html',
            categories=categories)
```

All the three handlers in the preceding code work in a similar way as discussed earlier with regard to rendering the product-related templates.

The following are all the templates created and rendered as a part of the application. To understand how these templates are written and how they work, refer to *Chapter 2, Templating with Jinja2.*

The flask_catalog_template/my_app/templates/home.html file looks as follows:

```
    {% extends 'base.html' %}

    {% block container %}
      <h1>Welcome to the Catalog Home</h1>
      <a href="{{ url_for('catalog.products') }}">Click here to see
        the catalog</a>
    {% endblock %}
```

The flask_catalog_template/my_app/templates/product.html file looks as follows:

```
    {% extends 'home.html' %}

    {% block container %}
      <div class="top-pad">
        <h1>{{ product.name }}<small> {{ product.category.name
          }}</small></h1>
        <h4>{{ product.company }}</h4>
        <h3>{{ product.price }}</h3>
      </div>
    {% endblock %}
```

The flask_catalog_template/my_app/templates/products.html file looks as follows:

```
    {% extends 'home.html' %}

    {% block container %}
```

```
<div class="top-pad">
  {% for product in products.items %}
    <div class="well">
      <h2>
        <a href="{{ url_for('catalog.product', id=product.id)
          }}">{{ product.name }}</a>
        <small>$ {{ product.price }}</small>
      </h2>
    </div>
  {% endfor %}
  {% if products.has_prev %}
    <a href="{{ url_for('catalog.products',
      page=products.prev_num) }}">
      {{"<< Previous Page"}}
    </a>
  {% else %}
    {{"<< Previous Page"}}
  {% endif %} |
  {% if products.has_next %}
    <a href="{{ url_for('catalog.products',
      page=products.next_num) }}">
      {{"Next page >>"}}
    </a>
  {% else %}
    {{"Next page >>"}}
  {% endif %}
</div>
{% endblock %}
```

The `flask_catalog_template/my_app/templates/category.html` file looks as follows:

```
{% extends 'home.html' %}

{% block container %}
  <div class="top-pad">
    <h2>{{ category.name }}</h2>
    <div class="well">
      {% for product in category.products %}
        <h3>
          <a href="{{ url_for('catalog.product', id=product.id) }}">{{
product.name }}</a>
          <small>$ {{ product.price }}</small>
        </h3>
```

```
    {% endfor %}
  </div>
 </div>
{% endblock %}
```

The `flask_catalog_template/my_app/templates/categories.html` file looks as follows:

```
{% extends 'home.html' %}

{% block container %}
  <div class="top-pad">
    {% for category in categories %}
    <a href="{{ url_for('catalog.category', id=category.id) }}">
      <h2>{{ category.name }}</h2>
    </a>
    {% endfor %}
  </div>
{% endblock %}
```

How it works...

Our view methods have a `render_template` method call at the end. This means that after the successful completion of the method operations, we will render a template with some parameters added to the context.

 Note how pagination has been implemented in the `products.html` file. It can be further improved to show the page numbers as well between the two links for navigation. I suggest that you try this out on your own.

See also

▶ Refer to the *URL routing and product-based pagination* recipe, to understand pagination and the rest of the application used in this recipe

Dealing with XHR requests

Asynchronous JavaScript XMLHttpRequest (XHR), commonly known as **Ajax,** has become an important part of web applications over the last few years. With the advent of one-page applications and JavaScript application frameworks such as **AngularJS**, **BackboneJS**, and more, this technique of web development has risen exponentially.

Getting ready

Flask provides an easy way to handle the XHR requests in the view handlers. We can even have common methods for normal web requests and XHRs. We can just look for a flag on our `request` object to determine the type of call and act accordingly.

We will update the catalog application from the previous recipe to have a feature that will demonstrate XHR requests.

How to do it...

The Flask `request` object has a flag called `is_xhr`, which tells us whether the request made is an XHR request or a simple web request. Usually, when we have an XHR request, the caller expects the result to be in the JSON format, which can then be used to render content at the correct place on the web page without reloading the page.

So, let's say we have an Ajax call to fetch the number of products in the database on the home page. One way to fetch the products is to send the count of products along with the `render_template()` context. Another way is to send this information over as the response to an Ajax call. We will implement the latter to understand how Flask handles XHR:

```python
from flask import request, render_template, jsonify


@catalog.route('/')
@catalog.route('/home')
def home():
    if request.is_xhr:
        products = Product.query.all()
        return jsonify({
            'count': len(products)
        })
    return render_template('home.html')
```

This design of handling XHR and regular requests together in one method can become a bit bloated, as the application grows large and different logic handling has to be done in the case of XHR in comparison to regular requests.

In such cases, these two types of requests can be separated into different methods where the handling of XHR is done separately from regular requests. This can even be extended to have different blueprints to make URL handling even cleaner.

In the preceding method, we first checked whether this is an XHR. If it is, we return the JSON data; otherwise, we just render `home.html` as we have done until now. First, modify `flask_catalog_template/my_app/templates/base.html` to a block for `scripts`. This empty block, which is shown here, can be placed after the line where the BootstrapJS script is included:

```
{% block scripts %}

{% endblock %}
```

Next, we have `flask_catalog_template/my_app/templates/home.html`, where we send an Ajax call to the `home()` handler, which checks whether the request is an XHR request. If it is, it fetches the count of products from the database and returns it as a JSON object. Check the code inside the `scripts` block:

```
{% extends 'base.html' %}

{% block container %}
    <h1>Welcome to the Catalog Home</h1>
    <a href="{{ url_for('catalog.products') }}" id="catalog_link">
      Click here to see the catalog
    </a>
{% endblock %}

{% block scripts %}
<script>
$(document).ready(function(){
    $.getJSON("/home", function(data) {
      $('#catalog_link').append('<span class="badge">' + data.count
        + '</span>');
    });
});
</script>
{% endblock %}
```

How it works...

Now, our home page contains a badge, which shows the number of products in the database. This badge will load only after the whole page has loaded. The difference in the loading of the badge and the other content on the page will be notable when the database has a considerably huge number of products.

The following screenshot shows how the home page looks now:

Decorator to handle requests beautifully

Some of us might think that checking whether a request is XHR or not every time kills code readability. To solve this, we have an easy solution. We can just write a simple decorator that will handle this redundant code for us.

Getting ready

In this recipe, we will be writing a decorator. For some of the beginners in Python, this might seem like alien territory. In this case, read `http://legacy.python.org/dev/peps/pep-0318/` for a better understanding of decorators.

How to do it...

The following is the decorator method that we have written for this recipe:

```python
from functools import wraps

def template_or_json(template=None):
    """Return a dict from your view and this will either
    pass it to a template or render json. Use like:

    @template_or_json('template.html')
    """
    def decorated(f):
        @wraps(f)
        def decorated_fn(*args, **kwargs):
            ctx = f(*args, **kwargs)
            if request.is_xhr or not template:
                return jsonify(ctx)
            else:
                return render_template(template, **ctx)
        return decorated_fn
    return decorated
```

This decorator simply does what we have done in the previous recipe to handle XHR, that is, checking whether our request is XHR and based on the outcome, either rendering the template or returning JSON data.

Now, let's apply this decorator to our `home()` method, which handled the XHR call in the previous recipe:

```
@app.route('/')
@app.route('/home')
@template_or_json('home.html')
def home():
    products = Product.query.all()
    return {'count': len(products)}
```

See also

▶ Refer to the *Dealing with XHR requests* recipe to understand how this recipe changes the coding pattern

▶ The reference for this recipe comes from `http://justindonato.com/notebook/template-or-json-decorator-for-flask.html`

Creating custom 404 and 500 handlers

Every application throws errors to users at some point of time. These errors can be due to the user typing a wrong URL (404), application overload (500), or something forbidden for a certain user to access (403). A good application handles these errors in an interactive way instead of showing an ugly white page, which makes no sense to most users. Flask provides an easy-to-use decorator to handle these errors.

Getting ready

The Flask `app` object has a method called `errorhandler()`, which enables us to handle our application's errors in a much more beautiful and efficient manner.

How to do it...

Consider the following code snippet:

```
@app.errorhandler(404)
def page_not_found(e):
    return render_template('404.html'), 404
```

Here, we have created a method that is decorated with `errorhandler()` and renders the `404.html` template whenever the **404 Not Found** error occurs.

The following lines of code represent the `flask_catalog_template/my_app/templates/404.html` template, which is rendered in the case of 404 errors:

```
{% extends 'home.html' %}

{% block container %}
  <div class="top-pad">
    <h3>Hola Friend! Looks like in your quest you have reached a
      location which does not exist yet.</h3>
    <h4>To continue, either check your map location (URL) or go
      back <a href="{{ url_for('catalog.home') }}">home</a></h4>
  </div>
{% endblock %}
```

How it works...

So, now, if we open a wrong URL, say `http://127.0.0.1:5000/i-am-lost`, then we will get what is shown in the following screenshot:

Similarly, we can add more error handlers for other error codes too.

There's more...

It is also possible to create custom errors as per the application requirements and bind them to error codes and custom error screens. This can be done as follows:

```
class MyCustom404(Exception):
    pass


@app.errorhandler(MyCustom404)
def special_page_not_found(error):
    return render_template("errors/custom_404.html"), 404
```

Flashing messages for better user feedback

An important part of all good web applications is to give users feedback about various activities. For example, when a user creates a product and is redirected to the newly created product, then it is a good practice to tell the user that the product has been created.

Getting ready

We will be adding the flash messages functionality to our existing catalog application. We also have to make sure that we add a secret key to the application, because the session depends on the secret key, and in the absence of the secret key, the application will error out while flashing.

How to do it...

To demonstrate the flashing of messages, we will flash messages on the creation of products. First, we will add a secret key to our app configuration in `flask_catalog_template/my_app/__init__.py`:

```
app.secret_key = 'some_random_key'
```

Now, we will modify our `create_product()` handler in `flask_catalog_template/my_app/catalog/views.py` to flash a message to the user about the product's creation. Also, a small change has been made to this handler where now, it will be possible to create the product from a web interface using a form:

```
from flask import flash

@catalog.route('/product-create', methods=['GET', 'POST'])
def create_product():
    if request.method == 'POST':
        name = request.form.get('name')
        price = request.form.get('price')
        categ_name = request.form.get('category')
        category = Category.query.filter_by
          (name=categ_name).first()
        if not category:
            category = Category(categ_name)
        product = Product(name, price, category)
        db.session.add(product)
        db.session.commit()
        flash('The product %s has been created' % name, 'success')
        return redirect(url_for('catalog.product', id=product.id))
    return render_template('product-create.html')
```

In the preceding method, we first checked whether the request type is POST. If yes, then we proceed to product creation as always or render the page with a form to create a new product. Also, notice the `flash` statement that will alert the user on the successful creation of a product. The first argument to `flash()` is the message to be displayed, and the second is the category of the message. We can use any identifier as suited in the message category. This can be used later to determine the type of alert message to be shown.

A new template is added; it holds the code for the product form. The path of the template will be `flask_catalog_template/my_app/templates/product-create.html`:

```
{% extends 'home.html' %}

{% block container %}
  <div class="top-pad">
    <form
        class="form-horizontal"
        method="POST"
        action="{{ url_for('catalog.create_product') }}"
        role="form">
      <div class="form-group">
        <label for="name" class="col-sm-2 control-
          label">Name</label>
        <div class="col-sm-10">
          <input type="text" class="form-control" id="name"
            name="name">
        </div>
      </div>
      <div class="form-group">
        <label for="price" class="col-sm-2 control-
          label">Price</label>
        <div class="col-sm-10">
          <input type="number" class="form-control" id="price"
            name="price">
        </div>
      </div>
      <div class="form-group">
        <label for="category" class="col-sm-2 control-
          label">Category</label>
        <div class="col-sm-10">
          <input type="text" class="form-control" id="category"
            name="category">
        </div>
      </div>
      <button type="submit" class="btn btn-
        default">Submit</button>
    </form>
  </div>
{% endblock %}
```

We will also modify our base template, that is, `flask_catalog_template/my_app/templates/base.html`, to accommodate flashed messages. Just add the following lines of code inside the `<div>` container before the `container` block:

```
<br/>
<div>
    {% for category, message in get_flashed_messages
       (with_categories=true) %}
      <div class="alert alert-{{category}} alert-dismissable">
        <button type="button" class="close" data-dismiss="alert"
          aria-hidden="true">&times;</button>
        {{ message }}
      </div>
    {% endfor %}
</div>
```

 Notice that in the `<div>` container, we have added a mechanism to show a flashed message that fetches the flashed messages in the template using `get_flashed_messages()`.

How it works...

A form, like the one shown in the following screenshot, will show up when you navigate to `http://127.0.0.1:5000/product-create`:

Flask Cookbook	
Name	
Price	
Category	
	Submit

Fill up the form and click on **Submit**. This will lead to the usual product page with an alert message at the top:

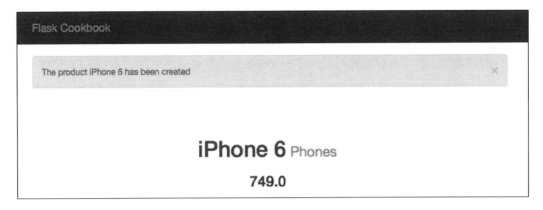

SQL-based searching

In any web application, it is important to be able to search the database for records based on some criteria. In this recipe, we will go through how to implement basic SQL-based searching in SQLAlchemy. The same principle can be used to search any other database system.

Getting ready

We have been implementing some level of search in our catalog application from the beginning. Whenever we show the product page, we search for a specific product using its ID. We will now take it to a more advanced level and search on the basis of name and category.

How to do it...

The following is a method that searches in our catalog application for name, price, company, and category. We can search for any one or multiple criterion (except for the search on category, which can only be searched alone). Notice that we have different expressions for different values. For a float value in price, we can search for equality, while in the case of a string, we can search using `like`. Also, carefully note how `join` is implemented in the case of category search. Place this method in the views file, that is, `flask_catalog_template/my_app/catalog/views.py`:

```
from sqlalchemy.orm.util import join

@catalog.route('/product-search')
@catalog.route('/product-search/<int:page>')
def product_search(page=1):
```

```
name = request.args.get('name')
price = request.args.get('price')
company = request.args.get('company')
category = request.args.get('category')
products = Product.query
if name:
    products = products.filter(Product.name.like('%' + name +
        '%'))
if price:
    products = products.filter(Product.price == price)
if company:
    products = products.filter(Product.company.like('%' +
        company + '%'))
if category:
    products = products.select_from(join(Product,
        Category)).filter(
            Category.name.like('%' + category + '%')
    )
return render_template(
    'products.html', products=products.paginate(page, 10)
)
```

How it works...

We can search for products by entering a URL, for example `http://127.0.0.1:5000/product-search?name=iPhone`. This will search for products with the name `iPhone` and list out the results on the `products.html` template. Similarly, we can search for price and/or company or category as needed. Try various combinations by yourself for a better understanding.

> We have used the same product list page to render our search results. It will be interesting to implement the search using Ajax. I will leave this to you to implement yourselves!

5
Webforms with WTForms

Form handling is an integral part of any web application. There can be innumerable cases that make the presence of forms in any web app very important. Some cases can be where users need to log in or submit some data or cases where applications might require input from users. As important as the forms are, their validation holds equal importance, if not more. Presenting this information to users in an interactive fashion adds a lot of value to the application.

In this chapter, we will cover the following recipes:

- ▶ SQLAlchemy model data as form representation
- ▶ Validating fields on the server side
- ▶ Creating a common forms set
- ▶ Creating custom fields and validation
- ▶ Creating a custom widget
- ▶ Uploading files via forms
- ▶ Cross-site Request Forgery protection

Introduction

There are various ways in which we can design and implement forms in a web application. With the advent of Web 2.0, form validation and communicating correct messages to the user has become very important. Client-side validations can be implemented at the frontend using JavaScript and HTML5. Server-side validations have a more important role in adding security to the application rather than being interactive. Server-side validations prevent any incorrect data from going through to the database and, hence, curb frauds and attacks.

WTForms provides a lot of fields with server-side validation by default and, hence, increases the development speed and decreases the overall effort. It also provides the flexibility to write custom validations and custom fields as needed.

We will use a Flask extension for this chapter. This extension is called Flask-WTF (`https://flask-wtf.readthedocs.org/en/latest/`); it provides a small integration between WTForms and Flask and takes care of important and simple stuff that we would have to otherwise reinvent in order to make our application secure and effective. We can install it using the following command:

```
$ pip install Flask-WTF
```

SQLAlchemy model data as form representation

First, let's build a form using a SQLAlchemy model. We will take the product model from our catalog application and add the functionality to create products from the frontend using a webform.

Getting ready

We will use our catalog application from *Chapter 4, Working with Views*. We will develop a form for the `Product` model.

How to do it...

To remind you, the `Product` model looks like the following lines of code in the `models.py` file:

```python
class Product(db.Model):
    id = db.Column(db.Integer, primary_key=True)
    name = db.Column(db.String(255))
    price = db.Column(db.Float)
    category_id = db.Column(db.Integer,
        db.ForeignKey('category.id'))
    category = db.relationship(
        'Category', backref=db.backref('products', lazy='dynamic')
    )
    company = db.Column(db.String(100))
```

First, we will create a `ProductForm` class; this will subclass the `Form` class, which is provided by `flask_wtf`, to represent the fields needed on a webform:

```
from flask_wtf import Form
from wtforms import TextField, DecimalField, SelectField

class ProductForm(Form):
    name = TextField('Name')
    price = DecimalField('Price')
    category = SelectField('Category', coerce=int)
```

We import `Form` from the `flask-wtf` extension. Everything else like `fields` and `validators` are imported from `wtforms` directly. The `Name` field is of type `TextField`, as it requires text data, while `Price` is of type `DecimalField`, which will parse the data to Python's `Decimal` datatype. We have kept `Category` as type `SelectField`, which means that we can choose only from the previously created categories while creating a product.

> Note that we have a parameter called `coerce` in the field definition for `Category` (which is a selection list); this means that the incoming data from the HTML form will be coerced into an integer value before validation or any other processing. Here, coercing simply means converting the value provided in a specific datatype to a different datatype.

The `create_product()` handler in `views.py` should now accommodate the form created earlier:

```
from my_app.catalog.models import ProductForm

@catalog.route('/product-create', methods=['GET', 'POST'])
def create_product():
    form = ProductForm(request.form, csrf_enabled=False)

    categories = [(c.id, c.name) for c in Category.query.all()]
    form.category.choices = categories

    if request.method == 'POST':
        name = request.form.get('name')
        price = request.form.get('price')
        category = Category.query.get_or_404(
            request.form.get('category')
        )
```

```
        product = Product(name, price, category)
        db.session.add(product)
        db.session.commit()
        flash('The product %s has been created' % name, 'success')
        return redirect(url_for('catalog.product', id=product.id))
    return render_template('product-create.html', form=form)
```

The `create_product()` method accepts values from a form on a POST request. This method will render an empty form with the prefilled choices in the `Category` field on a GET request. On the POST request, the form data will be used to create a new product, and when the creation of the product is completed, the newly created product's page will be displayed.

 You will notice that while creating the `form` object as `form = ProductForm(request.form, csrf_enabled=False)`, we set `csrf_enabled` to `False`. CSRF is an important part of any secure web application. We will talk about it in detail in the *Cross-site Request Forgery protection* recipe of this chapter.

The `templates/product-create.html` template also needs some modification too. The `form` objects created by WTForms provide an easy way to create HTML forms and keep the code readable:

```
{% extends 'home.html' %}

{% block container %}
  <div class="top-pad">
    <form method="POST" action="{{
      url_for('catalog.create_product') }}" role="form">
      <div class="form-group">{{ form.name.label }}: {{
        form.name() }}</div>
      <div class="form-group">{{ form.price.label }}: {{
        form.price() }}</div>
      <div class="form-group">{{ form.category.label }}: {{
        form.category() }}</div>
      <button type="submit" class="btn btn-
        default">Submit</button>
    </form>
  </div>
{% endblock %}
```

How it works...

On a GET request, that is, on opening `http://127.0.0.1:5000/product-create`, we will see a form similar to the one shown in the following screenshot:

You can fill in this form to create a new product.

See also

▶ The *Validating fields on the server side* recipe to understand how to validate the fields we just learned to create

Validating fields on the server side

We have forms and fields, but we need to validate them in order to make sure that only the correct data goes through to the database and errors are handled beforehand rather than corrupting the database. These validations can also prevent the application against **cross-site scripting** (**XSS**) and CSRF attacks. WTForms provides a whole lot of field types that themselves have validations written for them by default. Apart from these, there are a bunch of validators that can be used on the basis of choice and need. We will use a few of them to understand this concept further.

How to do it...

It is pretty easy to add validations to our WTForm fields. We just need to pass a `validators` parameter, which accepts a list of validators to be implemented. Each of the validators can have their own arguments, which enable us to control the validations to a great extent.

Let's modify our `ProductForm` class to have validations:

```
from decimal import Decimal
from wtforms.validators import InputRequired, NumberRange

class ProductForm(Form):
    name = TextField('Name', validators=[InputRequired()])
    price = DecimalField('Price', validators=[
        InputRequired(), NumberRange(min=Decimal('0.0'))
    ])
    category = SelectField(
        'Category', validators=[InputRequired()], coerce=int
    )
```

Here, we have the `InputRequired` validator on many fields; this means that these fields are required, and the form will not be submitted unless we have a value for these fields.

The `Price` field has an additional validator `NumberRange` with a `min` parameter set to 0. This implies that we cannot have a value less than 0 as the price of a product. To complement these changes, we will have to modify our `create_product()` method a bit:

```
@catalog.route('/product-create', methods=['GET', 'POST'])
def create_product():
    form = ProductForm(request.form, csrf_enabled=False)

    categories = [(c.id, c.name) for c in Category.query.all()]
    form.category.choices = categories

    if request.method == 'POST' and form.validate():
        name = form.name.data
        price = form.price.data
        category = Category.query.get_or_404(
            form.category.data
        )
        product = Product(name, price, category)
        db.session.add(product)
        db.session.commit()
        flash('The product %s has been created' % name, 'success')
        return redirect(url_for('product', id=product.id))

    if form.errors:
        flash(form.errors, 'danger')

    return render_template('product-create.html', form=form)
```

The flashing of `form.errors` will just display the errors in the form of a JSON object. This can be formatted to be shown in a pleasing format to the user. This is left for the users to try by themselves.

Here, we modified our `create_product()` method to validate the form for the input values and to check for the request method type. On a POST request, the form data will be validated first. If the validation fails for some reason, the same page will be rendered again, with error messages flashed on it. If the validation succeeds and the creation of the product is completed, the newly created product's page will be displayed.

How it works...

Now, try to submit the form without any field filled in, that is, an empty form. An alert message with an error will be shown as follows:

Try different combinations of form submission, which will violate the defined validators, and see the different error messages that come up.

There's more...

We can replace the processes of checking for the method type being a POST or PUT request and form validation with one step using `validate_on_submit`. So, the original code is:

```
if request.method == 'POST' and form.validate():
```

This can be replaced by:

```
if form.validate_on_submit():
```

> ▶ Refer to the previous recipe, *SQLAlchemy model data as form representation*, to understand basic form creation using WTForms

Creating a common forms set

An application can have loads of forms, depending on the design and purpose. Many of these forms will have common fields with common validators. Many of us might think, "Why not have common forms parts and then reuse them as and when needed?" This is very much possible with the class structure for forms' definition provided by WTForms.

How to do it...

In our catalog application, we can have two forms, one each for the `Product` and `Category` models. These forms will have a common field called `Name`. We can create a common form for this field, and then, the separate forms for the `Product` and `Category` models can use this form instead of having a `Name` field in each of them. This can be done as follows:

```
class NameForm(Form):
    name = TextField('Name', validators=[InputRequired()])


class ProductForm(NameForm):
    price = DecimalField('Price', validators=[
        InputRequired(), NumberRange(min=Decimal('0.0'))
    ])
    category = SelectField(
        'Category', validators=[InputRequired()], coerce=int
    )
    company = TextField('Company', validators=[Optional()])


class CategoryForm(NameForm):
    pass
```

We created a common form called `NameForm`, and the other forms, `ProductForm` and `CategoryForm`, inherit from this form to have a field called `Name` by default. Then, we can add more fields as needed.

We can modify the `category_create()` method to use `CategoryForm` to create categories:

```
@catalog.route('/category-create', methods=['GET', 'POST'])
def create_category():
    form = CategoryForm(request.form, csrf_enabled=False)

    if form.validate_on_submit():
        name = form.name.data
        category = Category(name)
        db.session.add(category)
        db.session.commit()
        flash('The category %s has been created' % name,
          'success')
        return redirect(url_for('catalog.category',
          id=category.id))

    if form.errors:
        flash(form.errors)

    return render_template('category-create.html', form=form)
```

A new template `templates/category-create.html` also needs to be added for category creation:

```
{% extends 'home.html' %}

{% block container %}
  <div class="top-pad">
    <form method="POST" action="{{
      url_for('catalog.create_category') }}" role="form">
      <div class="form-group">{{ form.name.label }}: {{
        form.name() }}</div>
      <button type="submit" class="btn btn-
        default">Submit</button>
    </form>
  </div>
{% endblock %}
```

How it works...

The newly created category form will look like the following screenshot:

Name: [   ]

Submit

 This is a very small example of how a common forms set can be implemented. The actual benefits of this approach can be seen in e-commerce applications, where we can have common address forms, and then, they can be expanded to have separate billing and shipment addresses.

Creating custom fields and validation

Apart from providing a bunch of fields and validations, Flask also provides the flexibility to create custom fields and validations. Sometimes, we might need to parse some form of data that cannot be processed using the available current fields. In such cases, we can implement our own fields.

How to do it...

In our catalog application, we used `SelectField` for the category, and we populated the values for this field in our `create_product()` method on a GET request. It would be much more convenient if we did not bother about this and the population of this field was taken care of by itself. Let's implement a custom field for this in `models.py`:

```
class CategoryField(SelectField):

    def iter_choices(self):
        categories = [(c.id, c.name) for c in
          Category.query.all()]
        for value, label in categories:
```

```
                yield (value, label, self.coerce(value) == self.data)

        def pre_validate(self, form):
            for v, _ in [(c.id, c.name) for c in
              Category.query.all()]:
                if self.data == v:
                    break
            else:
                raise ValueError(self.gettext('Not a valid choice'))

    class ProductForm(NameForm):
        price = DecimalField('Price', validators=[
            InputRequired(), NumberRange(min=Decimal('0.0'))
        ])
        category = CategoryField(
            'Category', validators=[InputRequired()], coerce=int
        )
```

`SelectField` implements a method called `iter_choices()`, which populates the values to the form using the list of values provided to the `choices` parameter. We overwrote the `iter_choices()` method to get the values of categories directly from the database, and this eliminates the need to populate this field every time we need to use this form.

> The behavior created by `CategoryField` here can also be achieved using `QuerySelectField`. Refer to `http://wtforms.readthedocs.org/en/latest/ext.html#wtforms.ext.sqlalchemy.fields.QuerySelectField` for more information.

Due to the changes described in this section, our `create_product()` method in `views.py` will have to be modified. For this, just remove the following two statements that populated the categories in the form:

```
categories = [(c.id, c.name) for c in Category.query.all()]
form.category.choices = categories
```

How it works...

There will not be any visual effect on the application. The only change will be in the way the categories are populated in the form, as explained in the previous section.

We just saw how to write custom fields. Similarly, we can write custom validations too. Let's assume that we do not want to allow duplicate categories. We can implement this in our models easily, but let's do this using a custom validator on our form:

```python
from wtforms.validators import ValidationError

def check_duplicate_category(case_sensitive=True):
    def _check_duplicate(form, field):
        if case_sensitive:
            res = Category.query.filter(
                Category.name.like('%' + field.data + '%')
            ).first()
        else:
            res = Category.query.filter(
                Category.name.ilike('%' + field.data + '%')
            ).first()
        if res:
            raise ValidationError(
                'Category named %s already exists' % field.data
            )
    return _check_duplicate

class CategoryForm(NameForm):
    name = TextField('Name', validators=[
        InputRequired(), check_duplicate_category()
    ])
```

So, we created our validator in a factory style, where we can get separate validation results based on whether we want a case-sensitive comparison or not. We can even write a class-based design, which makes the validator much more generic and flexible, but I will leave that for the readers to explore.

Creating a custom widget

Just like we can create custom fields and validators, we can also create custom widgets. These widgets allow us to control how our fields will look like at the frontend. Each field type has a widget associated with it. WTForms, by itself, provides a lot of basic and HTML5 widgets. To understand how to write a custom widget, we will convert our custom selection field for category into a radio field. I agree with many who would argue that we can directly use the radio field provided by WTForms. Here, we are just trying to understand how to do it ourselves.

The widgets provided by default by WTForms can be found at `https://wtforms.readthedocs.org/en/latest/widgets.html`.

How to do it...

In our previous recipe, we created `CategoryField`. This field used the `Select` widget, which was provided by the `Select` superclass. Let's replace the `Select` widget with a radio input:

```python
from wtforms.widgets import html_params, Select, HTMLString


class CustomCategoryInput(Select):

    def __call__(self, field, **kwargs):
        kwargs.setdefault('id', field.id)
        html = []
        for val, label, selected in field.iter_choices():
            html.append(
                '<input type="radio" %s> %s' % (
                    html_params(
                        name=field.name, value=val,
                        checked=selected, **kwargs
                    ), label
                )
            )
        return HTMLString(' '.join(html))

class CategoryField(SelectField):
    widget = CustomCategoryInput()

    # Rest of the code remains same as in last recipe Creating
    custom field and validation
```

Here, we added a class attribute called `widget` in our `CategoryField` class. This widget points to `CustomCategoryInput`, which takes care of HTML code generation for the field to be rendered. This class has a `__call__` method, which is overwritten to return radio inputs corresponding to the values provided by the `iter_choices()` method of `CategoryField`.

How it works...

When you open the product-creation page `http://127.0.0.1:5000/product-create`, it will look like the following screenshot:

Flask Cookbook
Name: [   ] Price: [   ] Category: ○ Phones ○ Tablets [Submit]

See also

> ▶ The previous recipe, *Creating custom fields and validation*, to understand more about the level of customization that can be done to the components of WTForms

Uploading files via forms

Uploading files via forms and doing it properly is usually a matter of concern for many web frameworks. Flask and WTForms handle this for us in a simple and streamlined manner.

How to do it...

First, we will start with the configuration bit. We need to provide a parameter to our application configuration, that is, UPLOAD_FOLDER. This parameter tells Flask about the location where our uploaded files will be stored. We will implement a feature to store product images.

 One way to store product images can be to store images in a binary type field in our database, but this method is highly inefficient and never recommended in any application. We should always store images and other uploads in the filesystem and store their location in the database using a string field.

Add the following statements to the configuration in `my_app/__init__.py`:

```
import os

ALLOWED_EXTENSIONS = set(['txt', 'pdf', 'png', 'jpg', 'jpeg', 'gif'])

app.config['UPLOAD_FOLDER'] = os.path.realpath('.') +
  '/my_app/static/uploads'
```

> Note the `app.config['UPLOAD_FOLDER']` statement where we store the images inside a subfolder in the `static` folder itself. This will make the process of rendering images easier. Also note the `ALLOWED_EXTENSIONS` statement that is used to make sure that only files of a specific format go through. The list here is actually for demonstration purposes only, and for image types, we can filter this list even more.

In the models file, that is, `my_app/catalog/models.py`, add the following highlighted statements in their designated places:

```
from wtforms import FileField

class Product(db.Model):
    image_path = db.Column(db.String(255))

    def __init__(self, name, price, category, image_path):
        self.image_path = image_path

class ProductForm(NameForm):
    image = FileField('Product Image')
```

Check `FileField` for image in `ProductForm` and the field for `image_path` in the `Product` model. This is in line with what we discussed earlier about storing files on the filesystem and storing their path in the DB.

Now, we can modify the `create_product()` method to save the file in `my_app/catalog/views.py`:

```
import os
from werkzeug import secure_filename
from my_app import ALLOWED_EXTENSIONS

def allowed_file(filename):
    return '.' in filename and \
```

```
                filename.lower().rsplit('.', 1)[1] in
                    ALLOWED_EXTENSIONS

    @catalog.route('/product-create', methods=['GET', 'POST'])
    def create_product():
        form = ProductForm(request.form, csrf_enabled=False)

        if form.validate_on_submit():
            name = form.name.data
            price = form.price.data
            category = Category.query.get_or_404(
                form.category.data
            )
            image = request.files['image']
            filename = ''
            if image and allowed_file(image.filename):
                filename = secure_filename(image.filename)
                image.save(os.path.join(app.config['UPLOAD_FOLDER'],
                    filename))
            product = Product(name, price, category, filename)
            db.session.add(product)
            db.session.commit()
            flash('The product %s has been created' % name, 'success')
            return redirect(url_for('catalog.product', id=product.id))

        if form.errors:
            flash(form.errors, 'danger')

        return render_template('product-create.html', form=form)
```

We need to add the new field to the `product-create` form in `template templates/product-create.html`. Modify the `form` tag definition to include the `enctype` parameter, and add the field for the image before the **Submit** button (or wherever you feel it is necessary inside the form):

```
<form method="POST"
    action="{{ url_for('create_product') }}"
    role="form"
    enctype="multipart/form-data">
<!-- The other field definitions as always -->
<div class="form-
    group">{{ form.image.label }}: {{
    form.image(style='display:inline;') }}</div>
```

The form should have the `enctype="multipart/form-data"` statement to tell the application that the form input will have multipart data.

Rendering the image is very easy as we are storing the files in the `static` folder. Just add the `img` tag wherever the image needs to be displayed in `templates/product.html`:

```
<img src="{{ url_for('static', filename='uploads/' +
    product.image_path) }}"/>
```

How it works...

The field to upload the image will look something like the following screenshot:

After the creation of the product, the image will be displayed as shown in the following screenshot:

Cross-site Request Forgery protection

In the first recipe of this chapter, we learned that CSRF is an important part of webform security. We will talk about it in detail now. CSRF stands for Cross-Site Request Forgery, which basically means that someone can hack into the request that carries a cookie and use this to trigger some destructive action. We won't be discussing CSRF in detail here, as ample resources are available on the Internet to learn about this. We will talk about how WTForms will help us in preventing CSRF. Flask does not provide any security from CSRF by default, as this has to be handled at the form validation level, which is not provided by Flask. However, this is done by the Flask-WTF extension for us.

 More about CSRF can be read at `http://en.wikipedia.org/wiki/Cross-site_request_forgery`.

How to do it...

Flask-WTF, by default, provides a form that is CSRF protected. If we have a look at the recipes so far, we will notice that we have explicitly told our form to *not be CSRF protected*. We just have to remove the corresponding statement to enable CSRF.

So, `form = ProductForm(request.form, csrf_enabled=False)` will become `form = ProductForm(request.form)`.

Some configuration bits also need to be done in our application:

```
app.config['WTF_CSRF_SECRET_KEY'] = 'random key for form'
```

By default, the CSRF key is the same as our application's secret key.

With CSRF enabled, we will have to provide an additional field in our forms; this is a hidden field and contains the CSRF token. WTForms takes care of the hidden field for us, and we just have to add `{{ form.csrf_token }}` to our form:

```
<form method="POST" action="/some-action-like-create-product">
    {{ form.csrf_token }}
</form>
```

That was easy! Now, this is not the only type of form submission that we do. We also submit AJAX form posts; this actually happens a lot more than normal forms with the advent of JS-based web applications, which are replacing traditional web applications.

For this, we have added an additional step in our application's configuration:

```
from flask_wtf.csrf import CsrfProtect


#
# Add configurations
#
CsrfProtect(app)
```

The preceding configuration will allow us to access the CSRF token using `{{ csrf_token() }}` anywhere in our templates. Now, there are two ways to add a CSRF token to AJAX POST requests.

One way is to fetch the CSRF token in our `script` tag and use it in the POST request:

```
<script type="text/javascript">
    var csrfToken = "{{ csrf_token() }}";
</script>
```

Another way is to render the token in a `meta` tag and use it whenever required:

```
<meta name="csrf-token" content="{{ csrf_token() }}"/>
```

The difference between both is that the first approach might have to be repeated at multiple places depending on the number of `script` tags in the application.

Now, to add the CSRF token to AJAX POST, we have to add the `X-CSRFToken` attribute to it. This attribute's value can be taken from any of the two approaches stated earlier. We will take the second one as our example:

```
var csrfToken = $('meta[name="csrf-token"]').attr('content');

$.ajaxSetup({
    beforeSend: function(xhr, settings) {
        if (!/^(GET|HEAD|OPTIONS|TRACE)$/i.test(settings.type)) {
            xhr.setRequestHeader("X-CSRFToken", csrftoken)
        }
    }
})
```

This will make sure that a CSRF token is added to all the AJAX POST requests that go out.

How it works...

The following screenshot shows what the CSRF token added by WTForms in our form looks like:

The token is completely random and different for all the requests. There are multiple ways of implementing CSRF-token generation, but this is out of the scope of this book, although I would encourage users to take a look at some implementations to understand how it's done.

6
Authenticating in Flask

Authentication is an important part of any application, be it web-based, desktop, or mobile. Each kind of application has certain best practices of handling user authentication. In web-based applications, especially SaaS-based applications, this process is of utmost importance, as it acts as the thin red line between the application being secure and unsecure.

In this chapter, we will cover the following recipes:

- ▶ Simple session-based authentication
- ▶ Authenticating using the Flask-Login extension
- ▶ Using OpenID for authentication
- ▶ Using Facebook for authentication
- ▶ Using Google for authentication
- ▶ Using Twitter for authentication

Introduction

To keep things simple and flexible, Flask, by default, does not provide a mechanism for authentication. It always has to be implemented by us, the developers, as per our and the application's requirements.

Authenticating users for your application can be done in multiple ways. It can be done using a simple session-based implementation or a more secure approach using the Flask-Login extension. We can also implement authentication by integrating with popular third-party services such as OpenID or social logins such as Facebook, Google, and so on. In this chapter, we will go through all of these methods.

Simple session-based authentication

In session-based authentication, when the user logs in for the first time, the user details are set in the session of the application's server side and stored in a cookie on the browser. After that, when the user opens the application, the details stored in the cookie are used to check against the session, and the user is automatically logged in if the session is alive.

 SECRET_KEY should always be specified in your application's configuration; otherwise, the data stored in the cookie as well as the session on the server side will be in plain text, which is highly unsecure.

We will implement a simple mechanism to do this ourselves.

 The implementation done in this recipe is only to explain how authentication basically works at a lower level. This approach should *not* be adopted in any production-level application.

Getting ready

We can start with a Flask app configuration as seen in *Chapter 5*, *Webforms with WTForms*. The application's configuration will be done to use the SQLAlchemy and WTForms extensions (refer to the previous chapter for details).

How to do it...

Before we start with the authentication, we need to have a model to store the user details. We will first create the models and forms in `flask_authentication/my_app/auth/models.py`:

```
from werkzeug.security import generate_password_hash,
    check_password_hash
from flask_wtf import Form
from wtforms import TextField, PasswordField
from wtforms.validators import InputRequired, EqualTo
from my_app import db


class User(db.Model):
    id = db.Column(db.Integer, primary_key=True)
    username = db.Column(db.String(100))
    pwdhash = db.Column(db.String())

    def __init__(self, username, password):
```

```
                self.username = username
                self.pwdhash = generate_password_hash(password)

        def check_password(self, password):
            return check_password_hash(self.pwdhash, password)
```

The preceding code is the `User` model, which has two fields: `username` and `pwdhash`. The `username` field works as its name suggests. The `pwdhash` field stores the salted hash of the password, because it is not recommended that you store passwords directly in databases.

Then, we will create two forms: one for user registration and the other for login. In `RegistrationForm`, we will create two fields of type `PasswordField`, just like any other website's registration; this is to make sure that the user enters the same password in both fields:

```
    class RegistrationForm(Form):
        username = TextField('Username', [InputRequired()])
        password = PasswordField(
            'Password', [
                InputRequired(), EqualTo('confirm', message='Passwords
                    must match')
            ]
        )
        confirm = PasswordField('Confirm Password', [InputRequired()])

    class LoginForm(Form):
        username = TextField('Username', [InputRequired()])
        password = PasswordField('Password', [InputRequired()])
```

Then, we will create views in `flask_authentication/my_app/auth/views.py` to handle the user requests for registration and login:

```
    from flask import request, render_template, flash, redirect,
      url_for, \
        session, Blueprint
    from my_app import app, db
    from my_app.auth.models import User, RegistrationForm, LoginForm

    auth = Blueprint('auth', __name__)

    @auth.route('/')
    @auth.route('/home')
    def home():
        return render_template('home.html')

    @auth.route('/register', methods=['GET', 'POST'])
    def register():
```

```
    if session.get('username'):
        flash('Your are already logged in.', 'info')
        return redirect(url_for('auth.home'))

form = RegistrationForm(request.form)

if request.method == 'POST' and form.validate():
    username = request.form.get('username')
    password = request.form.get('password')
    existing_username =
      User.query.filter_by(username=username).first()
    if existing_username:
        flash(
            'This username has been already taken. Try another
              one.',
            'warning'
        )
        return render_template('register.html', form=form)
    user = User(username, password)
    db.session.add(user)
    db.session.commit()
    flash('You are now registered. Please login.', 'success')
    return redirect(url_for('a
if form.errors:
    flash(form.errors, 'danger')

return render_template('register.html', form=form)
```

The preceding method handles user registration. On a GET request, the registration form is shown to the user; this form asks for the username and password. Then, the username is checked for its uniqueness after the form validation is complete. If the username is not unique, the user is asked to choose a new username; otherwise, a new user is created in the database and redirected to the login page, which is handled as shown in the following code:

```
@auth.route('/login', methods=['GET', 'POST'])
def login():
    form = LoginForm(request.form)

    if request.method == 'POST' and form.validate():
        username = request.form.get('username')
        password = request.form.get('password')
```

```
        existing_user =
          User.query.filter_by(username=username).first()

        if not (existing_user and existing_user.check_password
          (password)):
            flash('Invalid username or password. Please try
              again.', 'danger')
            return render_template('login.html', form=form)

        session['username'] = username
        flash('You have successfully logged in.', 'success')
        return redirect(url_for('auth.home'))

    if form.errors:
        flash(form.errors, 'danger')

    return render_template('login.html', form=form)
```

The preceding method handles the user login. After the form validation, we first check if
the username exists in the database. If not, we ask the user to enter the correct username.
Similarly, we check if the password is correct. If not, we ask the user for the correct password.
If all the checks pass, the session is populated with a `username` key, which holds the
username of the user. The presence of this key on the session indicates that the user is
logged in. Consider the following code:

```
@auth.route('/logout')
def logout():
    if 'username' in session:
        session.pop('username')
        flash('You have successfully logged out.', 'success')

    return redirect(url_for('auth.home'))
```

The preceding method becomes self-implied after we understand the `login()` method.
Here, we just popped out the `username` key from the session, and the user got logged
out automatically.

Then, we will create the templates that are rendered by the `register()` and `login()`
handlers for the registration and login, respectively, created earlier.

The `flask_authentication/my_app/templates/base.html` template remains almost
the same as it was in *Chapter 5, Webforms with WTForms*. The only change will be with the
routing where `catalog` will be replaced by `auth`.

First, we will have a simple home page `flask_authentication/my_app/templates/home.html`, which reflects if the user is logged in or not and shows links for registration and login if the user is not logged in:

```
{% extends 'base.html' %}

{% block container %}
  <h1>Welcome to the Authentication Demo</h1>
  {% if session.username %}
    <h3>Hey {{ session.username }}!!</h3>
    <a href="{{ url_for('auth.logout') }}">Click here to
      logout</a>
  {% else %}
  Click here to <a href="{{ url_for('auth.login') }}">login</a> or
      <a href="{{ url_for('auth.register') }}">register</a>
  {% endif %}
{% endblock %}
```

Then, we will create a registration page, `flask_authentication/my_app/templates/register.html`:

```
{% extends 'home.html' %}

{% block container %}
  <div class="top-pad">
    <form
        method="POST"
        action="{{ url_for('auth.register') }}"
        role="form">
      {{ form.csrf_token }}
      <div class="form-group">{{ form.username.label }}: {{
        form.username() }}</div>
      <div class="form-group">{{ form.password.label }}: {{
        form.password() }}</div>
      <div class="form-group">{{ form.confirm.label }}: {{
        form.confirm() }}</div>
      <button type="submit" class="btn btn-default">
        Submit</button>
    </form>
  </div>
{% endblock %}
```

Finally, we will create a simple login page, `flask_authentication/my_app/templates/login.html`:

```
{% extends 'home.html' %}

{% block container %}
  <div class="top-pad">
    <form
        method="POST"
        action="{{ url_for('auth.login') }}"
        role="form">
      {{ form.csrf_token }}
      <div class="form-group">{{ form.username.label }}: {{
        form.username() }}</div>
      <div class="form-group">{{ form.password.label }}: {{
        form.password() }}</div>
      <button type="submit" class="btn btn-default">
        Submit</button>
    </form>
  </div>
{% endblock %}
```

How it works...

How this application works is demonstrated with the help of the screenshots in this section.

The first screenshot is the home page that comes up on opening `http://127.0.0.1:5000/home`:

This is the home page visible to a user that is not logged in

The registration page that comes up on opening `http://127.0.0.1:5000/register` looks like the following screenshot:

The registration form

After the registration, the login page will be shown on opening `http://127.0.0.1:5000/login`:

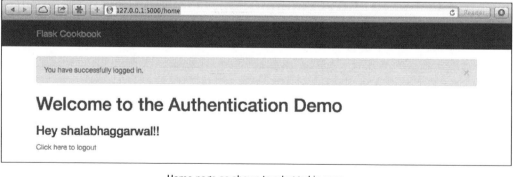

The login page rendered after successful registration

Finally, the home page is shown to the logged-in user at `http://127.0.0.1:5000/home`:

Home page as shown to a logged-in user

See also

▸ The next recipe, *Authenticating using the Flask-Login extension*, which covers a much secure and production-ready method of performing user authentication

Authenticating using the Flask-Login extension

In our previous recipe, we learned how to implement session-based authentication ourselves. Flask-Login is a popular extension that handles a lot of stuff for us in a very good way, saving us from reinventing the wheel all over again. It also does not bind us to any specific database or limit us to any specific fields/methods for authentication. It can also handle the *Remember me* feature, account recovery features, and so on.

Getting ready

We can modify the application created in the previous recipe to accommodate the changes to be done by the Flask-Login extension.

Before that, we have to install the extension itself:

```
$ pip install Flask-Login
```

How to do it...

To use Flask-Login, we have to first modify our application's configuration, which is in flask_authentication/my_app/__init__.py:

```
from flask.ext.login import LoginManager

#
# Do other application config
#

login_manager = LoginManager()
login_manager.init_app(app)
login_manager.login_view = 'login'
```

After importing the `LoginManager` class from the extension, we will create an object of this class. Then, we can configure the `app` object for use with `LoginManager` using `init_app()`. Then, we will have multiple configurations that can be done on our `login_manager` object as per our needs. Here, I have just demonstrated one basic and compulsory configuration, that is, `login_view`, which points to the view handler for our login requests. Further, we can even configure the messages to be shown to the users, how long our session will last, the app to handle logins using request headers, and so on. Refer to the Flask-Login documentation at `https://flask-login.readthedocs.org/en/latest/#customizing-the-login-process` for more details.

Flask-Login calls for some additional methods to be added to our `User` model/class:

```
def is_authenticated(self):
    return True

def is_active(self):
    return True

def is_anonymous(self):
    return False

def get_id(self):
    return unicode(self.id)
```

In the preceding code, we added four methods, which are explained as follows:

- `is_authenticated()`: This method usually returns `True`. This should return `False` only in cases where we do not want a user to be authenticated.
- `is_active()`: This method usually returns `True`. This should return `False` only in cases where we have blocked or banned a user.
- `is_anonymous()`: This method is used to indicate a user who is not supposed to be logged in to the system and should access the application as anonymous. This should usually return `False` for regular logged-in users.
- `get_id()`: This method represents the unique ID used to identify the user. This should be a unicode value.

Next, we have to make changes to our views in `my_app/views.py`:

```
from flask import g
from flask.ext.login import current_user, login_user, \
    logout_user, login_required
from my_app import login_manager

@login_manager.user_loader
def load_user(id):
```

```
        return User.query.get(int(id))

@auth.before_request
def get_current_user():
    g.user = current_user
```

In the preceding method, the `@auth.before_request` decorator implies that this method will be called before the view function whenever a request is received. Here, we have memoized our logged-in user:

```
@auth.route('/login', methods=['GET', 'POST'])
def login():
    if current_user.is_authenticated():
        flash('You are already logged in.')
        return redirect(url_for('auth.home'))

        # Same block of code as from last recipe Simple session
          based authentication
        # Next replace the statement session['username'] =
          username by the one below
        login_user(existing_user)
        flash('You have successfully logged in.', 'success')
        return redirect(url_for('auth.home'))

    if form.errors:
        flash(form.errors, 'danger')

    return render_template('login.html', form=form)

@auth.route('/logout')
@login_required
def logout():
    logout_user()
    return redirect(url_for('home'))
```

Notice that now, in `login()`, we checked if the `current_user` is authenticated before doing anything else. Here, `current_user` is a proxy to represent the object for the currently logged-in `User` record. Then, after all the validations and checks are done, the user is logged in using the `login_user()` method. This method accepts the user object and handles all the session-related activities to be done to log in a user.

Now, coming on to the `logout()` method, we first saw that there is a decorator added for `login_required()`. This decorator makes sure that the user is logged in before this method is executed. It can be used for any view method in our application. To log a user out, we just have to call `logout_user()`, which will clean up the session for the currently logged-in user and, in turn, log the user out of the application.

As we do not handle sessions ourselves, there will be a minor change in the templates too. This happens whenever we want to check if the user is logged in and there is some content to be shown based on this choice:

```
{% if current_user.is_authenticated() %}
...do something...
{% endif %}
```

How it works...

The demonstration in this recipe works exactly as it did in the previous recipe, *Simple session-based authentication*. Only the implementation differs, but the end result remains the same.

There's more...

The Flask-Login extension makes the implementation of the *Remember me* feature pretty simple. To do this, we just have to pass `remember=True` to the `login_user()` method. This will save a cookie on the user's computer, and Flask-Login will automatically use the same to log the user in automatically if the session is active. Readers should try implementing this on their own.

See also

- The previous recipe, *Simple session-based authentication*, to understand the complete working of this recipe.

- Flask provides a special object called g. You can read more about this at `http://flask.pocoo.org/docs/0.10/api/#flask.g`.

Using OpenID for authentication

OpenID allows us to use an existing account to sign in to multiple websites without the need to create new passwords for each website. Thus, this eliminates the need to share personal information with all the websites. There are certain cooperating sites (also known as **relying parties**) that authenticate user logins, and thousands of sites accept OpenID as an authentication mechanism. OpenID also allows you to control which information can be shared with the websites you visit and register with. Read more about OpenID and relying parties at `http://en.wikipedia.org/wiki/OpenID`.

Getting ready

Flask has an extension called **Flask-OpenID**, which makes the use and integration of OpenID with our application very simple and easy. This extension depends on the **python-openid** library. To install this, we can simply use the following command:

```
$ pip install Flask-OpenID
```

We will build over the application from the *Authenticating using the Flask-Login extension* recipe.

How to do it...

We will first start with our configuration in `flask_authentication/my_app/__init__.py`:

```python
from flask.ext.openid import OpenID

#
# Do other application config
#

oid = OpenID(app, 'openid-store')
```

First, we imported the `OpenID` class from the Flask extension. Then, we instantiated the class using our `app` object and created an object called `oid`. The second argument to `OpenID` while creating the `oid` object is the path to the store, which will store the OpenID information for the authentication process.

 Here, we used a path to a folder on the filesystem, but this can be configured to use your own store, which can be a relational database or a NoSQL document.

As we are integrating OpenID with our existing application keeping the existing functionality intact, we will use our existing `username` field to store the unique identifier received from OpenID, which can be `email` or `nickname`. This calls for the addition of a new form to our application to accept the OpenID URL:

```python
class OpenIDForm(Form):
    openid = TextField('OpenID', [InputRequired()])
```

The major chunk of changes will be to our views, that is, `flask_authentication/my_app/auth/views.py`:

```python
from my_app import oid
from my_app.auth.models import OpenIDForm


@auth.route('/login', methods=['GET', 'POST'])
@oid.loginhandler
def login():
    if g.user is not None and current_user.is_authenticated():
        flash('You are already logged in.', 'info')
        return redirect(url_for('home'))

    form = LoginForm(request.form)
    openid_form = OpenIDForm(request.form)

    if request.method == 'POST':
        if request.form.has_key('openid'):
            openid_form.validate()
            if openid_form.errors:
                flash(openid_form.errors, 'danger')
                return render_template(
                    'login.html', form=form,
                        openid_form=openid_form
                )
            openid = request.form.get('openid')
            return oid.try_login(openid, ask_for=['email',
                'nickname'])
        else:
            form.validate()
            if form.errors:
                flash(form.errors, 'danger')
                return render_template(
                    'login.html', form=form,
                        openid_form=openid_form
                )
            username = request.form.get('username')
            password = request.form.get('password')
            existing_user = User.query.filter_by
                (username=username).first()

            if not (existing_user and
                existing_user.check_password(password)):
                    flash(
```

```
                        'Invalid username or password. Please try
                            again.',
                        'danger'
                    )
                    return render_template('login.html', form=form)

            login_user(existing_user)
            flash('You have successfully logged in.', 'success')
            return redirect(url_for('auth.home'))

        if form.errors:
            flash(form.errors, 'danger')

        return render_template('login.html', form=form,
            openid_form=openid_form)
```

In the preceding method, we first checked if the current user is authenticated. If yes, then we redirect the user to the home page. Otherwise, if the request method is POST, then we first check if we have an openid field in our form. If there is such a field, we validate the OpenIDForm, and upon successful validation, we call oid.try_login(), which takes the OpenID URL and the fields to be fetched from the OpenID provider as the inputs. If the form does not have an openid field, then it is our regular form for a traditional login, and we follow the same process as we did in the previous recipe. Consider the following code:

```
@oid.after_login
def after_login(resp):
    username = resp.nickname or resp.email
    if not username:
        flash('Invalid login. Please try again.', 'danger')
        return redirect(url_for('auth.login'))
    user = User.query.filter_by(username=username).first()
    if user is None:
        user = User(username, '')
        db.session.add(user)
        db.session.commit()
    login_user(user)
    return redirect(url_for('auth.home'))
```

This method is called after OpenID's try_login() method receives a response from the provider. All this happens asynchronously. First, we tried to fetch the nickname or email from the provider. If none of the two are found, then this login is invalid. Then, we checked for an existing user with the nickname or email by matching in the username field. If a user is found, we log the user in; otherwise, we create a new user and then log in.

This also calls for a small change in our `templates/login.html` template to accommodate `OpenIDForm`:

```
{% extends 'home.html' %}

{% block container %}
  <div class="top-pad">
    <ul class="nav nav-tabs">
      <li class="active"><a href="#simple-form" data-
        toggle="tab">Old Style Login</a></li>
      <li><a href="#openid-form" data-toggle="tab">OpenID</a></li>
    </ul>
    <div class="tab-content">
      <div class="tab-pane active" id="simple-form">
        <form
            method="POST"
            action="{{ url_for('auth.login') }}"
            role="form">
          {{ form.csrf_token }}
          <div class="form-group">{{ form.username.label }}: {{
            form.username() }}</div>
          <div class="form-group">{{ form.password.label }}: {{
            form.password() }}</div>
          <button type="submit" class="btn btn-
            default">Submit</button>
        </form>
      </div>
      <div class="tab-pane" id="openid-form">
        <form
            method="POST"
            action="{{ url_for('auth.login') }}"
            role="form">
          {{ openid_form.csrf_token }}
          <div class="form-group">{{ openid_form.openid.label }}:
            {{ openid_form.openid() }}</div>
          <button type="submit" class="btn btn-
            default">Submit</button>
        </form>
      </div>
    </div>
  </div>
{% endblock %}
```

In this code, we created a tabbed structure where the first tab is our conventional login and the second tab corresponds to the OpenID login.

How it works...

The tabbed page for login will look like the following screenshot:

We have to enter an OpenID URL, and the rest of the process will work according to the provider.

Using Facebook for authentication

We have seen that many websites provide an option to log in to their website using third-party authentications such as Facebook, Google, Twitter, LinkedIn, and so on. This has been made possible by OAuth, which is an open standard for authorization. It allows the client site to use an access token to access the protected information/resources provided by the resource server. In this recipe, we will see how to implement OAuth-based authorization via Facebook. In the recipes to follow, we will do the same using other providers.

Getting started

First, we will start by installing the Flask-OAuth extension and its dependencies:

```
$ pip install Flask-OAuth
```

Next, we have to register for a Facebook application that will be used for login. Although the process for registration with the Facebook app is pretty straightforward and self-explanatory, we are only concerned with the **App ID**, **App Secret**, and **Site URL** options. The following screenshot should help you in understanding this. More details can be found on the Facebook developer pages at `https://developers.facebook.com/`.

How to do it...

As always, we will first start with the configuration part in `my_app/__init__.py`:

```python
from flask_oauth import OAuth

oauth = OAuth()

facebook = oauth.remote_app('facebook',
    base_url='https://graph.facebook.com/',
    request_token_url=None,
    access_token_url='/oauth/access_token',
    authorize_url='https://www.facebook.com/dialog/oauth',
    consumer_key='FACEBOOK_APP_ID',
    consumer_secret='FACEBOOK_APP_SECRET',
    request_token_params={'scope': 'email'}
)
```

In the previous code snippet, we registered a remote Facebook application with our application for authentication. All the parameters passed in `remote_app()` will remain the same for all the Facebook remote apps except `consumer_key` and `consumer_secret`, which actually correspond to the **App ID** and **App Secret** options, respectively, of our Facebook application.

Next, we will modify our views, that is, `my_app/auth/views.py`:

```
from my_app import facebook

@auth.route('/facebook-login')
def facebook_login():
    return facebook.authorize(
        callback=url_for(
            'auth.facebook_authorized',
            next=request.args.get('next') or request.referrer or
                None,
            _external=True
        ))
```

The previous method calls the `authorize()` method of the `OAuth` instance with a callback URL to which the response received from Facebook should be passed for further action.

> The `_external=True` statement here implies that the URL can be external to the application.

Consider the following code:

```
@auth.route('/facebook-login/authorized')
@facebook.authorized_handler
def facebook_authorized(resp):
    if resp is None:
        return 'Access denied: reason=%s error=%s' % (
            request.args['error_reason'],
            request.args['error_description']
        )
    session['facebook_oauth_token'] = (resp['access_token'], '')
    me = facebook.get('/me')
    user = User.query.filter_by(username=me.data['email']).first()
    if not user:
        user = User(me.data['email'], '')
```

```
        db.session.add(user)
        db.session.commit()

    login_user(user)
    flash(
        'Logged in as id=%s name=%s' % (me.data['id'],
          me.data['name']),
        'success'
    )
    return redirect(request.args.get('next'))
```

The previous method handles the response received from Facebook and logs the user in, if the user with the same e-mail address already exists; otherwise, it creates a new user and then logs the user in. Consider the following code:

```
@facebook.tokengetter
def get_facebook_oauth_token():
    return session.get('facebook_oauth_token')
```

This method just fetches the token that is stored in the session for the current user.

Finally, we will modify our login template to allow the Facebook login. First, we add a tab for social logins:

```
<ul class="nav nav-tabs">
    <li class="active"><a href="#simple-form" data-toggle="tab">Old
Style Login</a></li>
    <li><a href="#openid-form" data-toggle="tab">OpenID</a></li>
    <li><a href="#social-logins" data-toggle="tab">Social Logins</
a></li>
    </ul>
```

This is followed by adding the contents for the newly added **Social** logins tab:

```
<div class="tab-pane" id="social-logins">
    <a href="{{ url_for('auth.facebook_login',
        next=url_for('auth.home')) }}">Login via Facebook</a>
</div>
```

So, we just added a new tab to allow social logins. Right now, we have just one for Facebook here. More will be added in the recipes to follow. Also, we just have a simple link right now; we can always add styles and buttons as needed.

How it works...

The login page has a new tab that provides an option to the user to log in using social logins:

When we click on the **Login via Facebook** link, the application will be taken to Facebook and will ask for user login and permission. Once the permission is granted, the user will be logged in to the application.

Using Google for authentication

Just like we did for Facebook, we can integrate our application to enable login using Google.

Getting ready

We will start by building over the last recipe. It is easy to just implement Google authentication by leaving out the Facebook auth (by leaving out the Facebook-specific parts).

Now, we have to create a project from the Google developer console (`https://console.developers.google.com`). Then, we have to create a client ID for the web application; this ID will provide the credentials needed for OAuth to work. The following screenshot should help:

How to do it...

As always, we will first start with the configuration part in `my_app/__init__.py`:

```python
from flask_oauth import OAuth

oauth = OAuth()

google = oauth.remote_app('google',
    base_url='https://www.google.com/accounts/',
    authorize_url='https://accounts.google.com/o/oauth2/auth',
    request_token_url=None,
    request_token_params={
        'scope': 'https://www.googleapis.com/auth/userinfo.email',
        'response_type': 'code'
    },
    access_token_url='https://accounts.google.com/o/oauth2/token',
    access_token_method='POST',
    access_token_params={'grant_type': 'authorization_code'},
    consumer_key='GOOGLE_CLIENT_ID',
    consumer_secret='GOOGLE_CLIENT_SECRET'
)
```

In the preceding code, we registered a remote Google application with our application for authentication. All the parameters passed in `remote_app()` will remain the same for all the Google remote apps except `consumer_key` and `consumer_secret`, which actually correspond to the **Client ID** and **Client secret** options, respectively, of our Google project.

Next, we will modify our views, that is, `my_app/auth/views.py`:

```python
import requests
from my_app import google

GOOGLE_OAUTH2_USERINFO_URL = \
    'https://www.googleapis.com/oauth2/v1/userinfo'

@auth.route('/google-login')
def google_login():
    return google.authorize(
        callback=url_for('auth.google_authorized',
          _external=True))
```

The preceding method calls the `authorize()` method of the `OAuth` instance with a callback URL to which the response received from Google should be passed for further action. Consider the following code:

```python
@auth.route('/oauth2callback')
@google.authorized_handler
def google_authorized(resp):
    if resp is None:
        return 'Access denied: reason=%s error=%s' % (
            request.args['error_reason'],
            request.args['error_description']
        )
    session['google_oauth_token'] = (resp['access_token'], '')
    userinfo = requests.get(GOOGLE_OAUTH2_USERINFO_URL,
      params=dict(
        access_token=resp['access_token'],
    )).json()

    user = User.query.filter_by(username=userinfo
      ['email']).first()
    if not user:
        user = User(userinfo['email'], '')
        db.session.add(user)
        db.session.commit()

    login_user(user)
    flash(
        'Logged in as id=%s name=%s' % (userinfo['id'],
          userinfo['name']),
        'success'
    )
    return redirect(url_for('auth.home'))
```

The preceding method handles the response received from Google and logs the user in if a user with the same e-mail address already exists; otherwise, it creates a new user and then logs the user in. An important point to note here is that the route URL of this method is the same as the redirect URL set in our Google client settings (see the *Getting ready* section of this recipe). Consider the following code:

```python
@google.tokengetter
def get_google_oauth_token():
    return session.get('google_oauth_token')
```

This method just fetches the token that is stored in the session for the current user. Finally, we will modify our login template to allow the Google login:

```
<a href="{{ url_for('auth.google_login') }}">Login via Google</a>
```

How it works...

The Google login works in a manner similar to how the Facebook login from the previous recipe works.

Using Twitter for authentication

OAuth was actually born while writing the OpenID API for Twitter. In this recipe, we will integrate Twitter login with our application.

Getting ready

We will continue by building over the *Using Google for authentication* recipe. It is easy to just implement Twitter auth by leaving out specific parts from Facebook and/or Google authentication.

Now, we have to create an application from the Twitter **Application Management** page (`https://apps.twitter.com/`). It will automatically create **API key** and **API secret** for us to use. Have a look at the following screenshot:

How to do it...

As always, we will first start with the configuration part in `my_app/__init__.py`:

```
from flask_oauth import OAuth

oauth = OAuth()

twitter = oauth.remote_app('twitter',
    base_url='https://api.twitter.com/1.1/',
    request_token_url='https://api.twitter.com/oauth/request_token',
    access_token_url='https://api.twitter.com/oauth/access_token',
    authorize_url='https://api.twitter.com/oauth/authenticate',
    consumer_key='Twitter API Key',
    consumer_secret='Twitter API Secret'
)
```

In the preceding code, we registered a remote Twitter application with our application for authentication. All the parameters passed in `remote_app()` will remain the same for all Twitter remote apps except `consumer_key` and `consumer_secret`, which actually correspond to the **API key** and **API secret** options, respectively, of our Twitter application.

Next, we will modify our views, that is, `my_app/auth/views.py`:

```
from my_app import twitter

@auth.route('/twitter-login')
def twitter_login():
    return twitter.authorize(
        callback=url_for(
            'auth.twitter_authorized',
            next=request.args.get('next') or request.referrer or
                None,
            _external=True
        ))
```

The preceding method calls the `authorize()` method of the `OAuth` instance with a callback URL to which the response received from Twitter should be passed for further action. Consider the following code:

```
@auth.route('/twitter-login/authorized')
@twitter.authorized_handler
def twitter_authorized(resp):
    if resp is None:
        return 'Access denied: reason=%s error=%s' % (
            request.args['error_reason'],
```

```
            request.args['error_description']
        )
    session['twitter_oauth_token'] = resp['oauth_token'] + \
            resp['oauth_token_secret']

    user = User.query.filter_by(username=resp
      ['screen_name']).first()
    if not user:
        user = User(resp['screen_name'], '')
        db.session.add(user)
        db.session.commit()

    login_user(user)
    flash('Logged in as twitter handle=%s' % resp['screen_name'])
    return redirect(request.args.get('next'))
```

The preceding method handles the response received from Twitter and logs the user in if a user with same Twitter screen name (also known as a Twitter handle) already exists; otherwise, it creates a new user and then logs the user in. Consider the following code:

```
@twitter.tokengetter
def get_twitter_oauth_token():
    return session.get('twitter_oauth_token')
```

This method just fetches the token that is stored in the session for the current user. Finally, we will modify our login template to allow the Twitter login:

```
<a href="{{ url_for('auth.twitter_login',
    next=url_for('auth.home')) }}">Login via Twitter</a>
```

How it works...

This recipe works in a manner similar to how the Facebook and Google logins from the previous recipes work.

> Similarly, we can integrate LinkedIn, GitHub, and scores of other third-party providers that provide support for login and authentication using OAuth. I will leave it to you to implement many more integrations on your own. The following links have been added for quick reference:
>
> ▸ **LinkedIn**: `https://developer.linkedin.com/documents/authentication`
>
> ▸ **GitHub**: `https://developer.github.com/v3/oauth/`

7
RESTful API Building

An API, or Application Programming Interface, can be summarized as a developer's interface to the application. Just like end users have a visible frontend user interface to work on and talk to the application, developers also need a user interface to the application. REST, or REpresentational State Transfer, is not a protocol or a standard. It is just a software architectural style or a set of constraints defined for writing applications and aims at simplifying the interfaces within and outside the application. When web service APIs are written in a way to adhere to the REST constraints, then they are known as RESTful APIs. Being RESTful keeps the API decoupled from the internal application details. This results in ease of scalability and keeps things simple. The uniform interface ensures that each and every request is documented.

 It is a topic of debate whether REST is better or SOAP is. It actually is a subjective question as it depends on what needs to be done. Each has its own benefits and should be chosen as per the needs of the application.

In this chapter, we will cover the following recipes:

- ▸ Creating a class-based REST interface
- ▸ Creating an extension-based REST interface
- ▸ Creating a SQLAlchemy-independent REST API
- ▸ A complete REST API example

Introduction

As the name suggests, **REpresentational State Transfer** (**REST**) calls for segregating your API into logical resources, which can be accessed and manipulated using HTTP requests, where each request consists of a method out of GET, POST, PUT, PATCH, and DELETE (there can be more, but these are the ones used the most). Each of these methods has a specific meaning. One of the key implied principles of REST is that the logical grouping of resources should be easily understandable and, hence, provide simplicity along with portability.

Up until now in this book, we have used a resource called Product. Let's see how we can logically map our API calls to the resource segregation:

- ► `GET /products/1`: This gets the product with ID `1`
- ► `GET /products`: This gets the list of products
- ► `POST /products`: This creates a new product
- ► `PUT /products/1`: This updates the product with ID `1`
- ► `PATCH /products/1`: This partially updates the product with ID `1`
- ► `DELETE /products/1`: This deletes the product with ID `1`

Creating a class-based REST interface

We saw how class-based views work in Flask using the concept of pluggable views in the *Class-based views* recipe in *Chapter 4, Working with Views*. We will now see how we can use the same concept to create views, which will provide a REST interface to our application.

Getting ready

Let's take a simple view that will handle the REST style calls to our `Product` model.

How to do it...

We have to simply modify our views for product handling to extend the `MethodView` class:

```python
from flask.views import MethodView

class ProductView(MethodView):

    def get(self, id=None, page=1):
        if not id:
            products = Product.query.paginate(page, 10).items
            res = {}
```

```
        for product in products:
            res[product.id] = {
                'name': product.name,
                'price': product.price,
                'category': product.category.name
            }
    else:
        product = Product.query.filter_by(id=id).first()
        if not product:
            abort(404)
        res = json.dumps({
            'name': product.name,
            'price': product.price,
            'category': product.category.name
        })
    return res
```

The preceding `get()` method searches for the product and sends back a JSON result.

Similarly, we can write the `post()`, `put()`, and `delete()` methods too:

```
def post(self):
    # Create a new product.
    # Return the ID/object of newly created product.
    return

def put(self, id):
    # Update the product corresponding provided id.
    # Return the JSON corresponding updated product.
    return

def delete(self, id):
    # Delete the product corresponding provided id.
    # Return success or error message.
    return
```

Many of us would wonder why we have no routing here. To include routing, we have to do the following:

```
product_view = ProductView.as_view('product_view')
app.add_url_rule('/products/', view_func=product_view,
    methods=['GET', 'POST'])
app.add_url_rule('/products/<int:id>', view_func=product_view,
    methods=['GET', 'PUT', 'DELETE'])
```

The first statement here converts the class to an actual view function internally that can be used with the routing system. The next two statements are the URL rules corresponding to the calls that can be made.

How it works...

The `MethodView` class identified the type of HTTP method in the request sent and converted the name to lowercase. Then, it matched this to the methods defined in the class and called the matched method. So, if we make a GET call to `ProductView`, it will automatically be mapped to the `get()` method and processed accordingly.

There's more...

We can also use a Flask extension for this called Flask-Classy (`https://pythonhosted.org/Flask-Classy/`). This will handle the classes and routing automatically to a great extent and make life easier. We won't be discussing this here though, but it's an extension that is definitely worth exploring.

Creating an extension-based REST interface

In the previous recipe, *Creating a class-based REST interface*, we saw how to create a REST interface using pluggable views. Here, we will use a Flask extension, Flask-Restless, developed completely from the point of view of building REST interfaces. It provides a simple generation of RESTful APIs for database models defined using SQLAlchemy. These generated APIs send and receive messages in the JSON format.

Getting ready

First, we need to install the Flask-Restless extension:

```
$ pip install Flask-Restless
```

We will build over our application from the *SQL-based searching* recipe of *Chapter 4, Working with Views*, to include a RESTful API interface.

 It is advisable that you read *Chapter 4, Working with Views*, before moving ahead if the concepts of views and handlers are not clear.

How to do it...

Adding a RESTful API interface to a SQLAlchemy model is very easy with the use of Flask-Restless. First, we need to add the REST API manager provided by this extension to our application config and create an instance of it using the `app` object:

```
from flask.ext.restless import APIManager

manager = APIManager(app, flask_sqlalchemy_db=db)
```

After this, we need to enable API creation on our models using the `manager` instance. For this, we can just add the following lines of code to `views.py`:

```
from my_app import manager

manager.create_api(Product, methods=['GET', 'POST', 'DELETE'])
manager.create_api(Category, methods=['GET', 'POST', 'DELETE'])
```

This will create RESTful APIs with the GET, POST, and DELETE methods on our models for `Product` and `Category`. By default, only the GET method is provided if the `methods` argument is missed out.

How it works...

To test and see how this works, we can send some `requests` using the Python shell using the requests library:

```
>>> import requests
>>> import json
>>> res = requests.get('http://127.0.0.1:5000/api/category')
>>> res.json()
{u'total_pages': 0, u'objects': [], u'num_results': 0, u'page': 1}
```

We made a GET request to fetch a list of categories, but right now, there is no record for it. Let's look for the products now:

```
>>> res = requests.get('http://127.0.0.1:5000/api/product')
>>> res.json()
{u'total_pages': 0, u'objects': [], u'num_results': 0, u'page': 1}
```

We made a GET request to fetch the list of products, but there is no record for it. Let's create a new product now:

```
>>> d = {'name': u'iPhone', 'price': 549.00, 'category':
{'name':'Phones'}}
>>> res = requests.post('http://127.0.0.1:5000/api/product', data=json.
dumps(d), headers={'Content-Type': 'application/json'})
>>> res.json()
{u'category': {u'id': 1, u'name': u'Phones'}, u'name': u'iPhone',
u'company': u'', u'price': 549.0, u'category_id': 1, u'id': 2, u'image_
path': u''}
```

We sent a POST request to create a product with some data. Notice the `headers` argument in the request. Each POST request sent in Flask-Restless should have this header. Now, we should look for the list of products again:

```
>>> res = requests.get('http://127.0.0.1:5000/api/product')
>>> res.json()
{u'total_pages': 1, u'objects': [{u'category': {u'id': 1, u'name':
u'Phones'}, u'name': u'iPhone', u'company': u'', u'price': 549.0,
u'category_id': 1, u'id': 1, u'image_path': u''}], u'num_results': 1,
u'page': 1}
```

If we look for the products again via a GET request, we can see that we have a newly created product in the database now.

Also notice that the results are already paginated by default; this is one of the signs of a good API design.

There's more...

This automatic creation of a RESTful API interface is cool, but every application needs some customizations, validations, and handling of requests as per the application business logic. This is made possible using request `preprocessors` and `postprocessors`. As evident by the names, `preprocessors` are the methods that will run before the request is processed, and `postprocessors` run after the request is processed and before the response is sent by the application. These are defined in `create_api()` as maps of the request type (GET, POST, and so on) and the list of methods to act as `preprocessors` or `postprocessors` on the specified request:

```
    manager.create_api(
        Product,
        methods=['GET', 'POST', 'DELETE'],
        preprocessors={
            'GET_SINGLE': ['a_preprocessor_for_single_get'],
            'GET_MANY': ['another_preprocessor_for_many_get'],
```

```
            'POST': ['a_preprocessor_for_post']
    },
    postprocessors={
        'DELETE': ['a_postprocessor_for_delete']
    }
)
```

The GET, PUT, and PATCH requests can be called for single or multiple records; hence, they have two variants each. For example, in the preceding code, we have GET_SINGLE and GET_MANY for GET requests. The preprocessors and postprocessors for each of the request type accept different arguments and act upon them without returning any return value. Refer to the Flask-Restless documentation at https://flask-restless.readthedocs.org/en/latest/ at for more details.

Creating a SQLAlchemy-independent REST API

In the previous recipe, *Creating an extension-based REST interface*, we saw how to create a REST API interface using an extension that was dependent on SQLAlchemy. Now, we will use an extension called Flask-Restful, which is written over Flask pluggable views and is independent of ORM.

Getting ready

First, we will start with the installation of the extension:

$ pip install Flask-Restful

We will modify the catalog application from the previous recipe to add a REST interface using this extension.

How to do it...

As always, we will start with changes to our application's configuration, which will look something like the following lines of code:

```
from flask.ext.restful import Api

api = Api(app)
```

Here, app is our Flask application object/instance.

Next, we will create our API inside the `views.py` file. Here, we will just try to understand how to lay out the skeleton of the API. Actual methods and handlers will be covered in the *A complete REST API example* recipe:

```python
from flask.ext.restful import Resource
from my_app import api

class ProductApi(Resource):

    def get(self, id=None):
        # Return product data
        return 'This is a GET response'

    def post(self):
        # Create a new product
        return 'This is a POST response'

    def put(self, id):
        # Update the product with given id
        return 'This is a PUT response'

    def delete(self, id):
        # Delete the product with given id
        return 'This is a DELETE response'
```

The preceding API structure is self-explanatory. Consider the following code:

```python
api.add_resource(
    ProductApi,
    '/api/product',
    '/api/product/<int:id>'
)
```

Here, we created the routing for `ProductApi`, and we can specify multiple routes as needed.

How it works...

We will see how this will work on the Python shell using the `requests` library just like we did in the previous recipe:

```python
>>> import requests
>>> res = requests.get('http://127.0.0.1:5000/api/product')
>>> res.json()
u'This is a GET response'
>>> res = requests.post('http://127.0.0.1:5000/api/product')
```

```
u'This is a POST response'
>>> res = requests.put('http://127.0.0.1:5000/api/product/1')
u'This is a PUT response'
>>> res = requests.delete('http://127.0.0.1:5000/api/product/1')
u'This is a DELETE response'
```

In the preceding snippet, we saw that all our requests are properly routed to the respective methods; this is evident from the response received.

See also

▶ Make sure you read the next recipe, *A complete REST API example*, to see the API skeleton from this recipe coming to life

A complete REST API example

In this recipe, we will convert the API structure created in the previous recipe, *Creating a SQLAlchemy-independent REST API*, into a full-fledged RESTful API interface.

Getting ready

We will take the API skeleton from the previous recipe as the base to create a complete functional SQLAlchemy-independent RESTful API. Although we will use SQLAlchemy as the ORM for demonstration, this recipe can be written in a similar fashion for any ORM or underlying database.

How to do it...

The following lines of code are the complete RESTful API for the `Product` model. These code snippets will go into the `views.py` file:

```
from flask.ext.restful import reqparse

parser = reqparse.RequestParser()
parser.add_argument('name', type=str)
parser.add_argument('price', type=float)
parser.add_argument('category', type=dict)
```

In the preceding snippet, we created `parser` for the arguments that we expected to have in our requests for POST and PUT. The request expects each of the argument to have a value. If a value is missing for any argument, then `None` is used as the value. Consider the following code:

```
class ProductApi(Resource):

    def get(self, id=None, page=1):
        if not id:
            products = Product.query.paginate(page, 10).items
        else:
            products = [Product.query.get(id)]
        if not products:
            abort(404)
        res = {}
        for product in products:
            res[product.id] = {
                'name': product.name,
                'price': product.price,
                'category': product.category.name
            }
        return json.dumps(res)
```

The preceding `get()` method corresponds to GET requests and returns a paginated list of products if no `id` is passed; otherwise, it returns the corresponding product. Consider the following code:

```
    def post(self):
        args = parser.parse_args()
        name = args['name']
        price = args['price']
        categ_name = args['category']['name']
        category = Category.query.filter_by
          (name=categ_name).first()
        if not category:
            category = Category(categ_name)
        product = Product(name, price, category)
        db.session.add(product)
        db.session.commit()
        res = {}
        res[product.id] = {
            'name': product.name,
            'price': product.price,
            'category': product.category.name,
        }
        return json.dumps(res)
```

The preceding `post()` method will lead to the creation of a new product by making a POST request. Consider the following code:

```
def put(self, id):
    args = parser.parse_args()
    name = args['name']
    price = args['price']
    categ_name = args['category']['name']
    category = Category.query.filter_by
        (name=categ_name).first()
    Product.query.filter_by(id=id).update({
        'name': name,
        'price': price,
        'category_id': category.id,
    })
    db.session.commit()
    product = Product.query.get_or_404(id)
    res = {}
    res[product.id] = {
        'name': product.name,
        'price': product.price,
        'category': product.category.name,
    }
    return json.dumps(res)
```

In the preceding code, we updated an existing product using a PUT request. Here, we should provide all the arguments even if we intend to change a few of them. This is because of the conventional way in which PUT has been defined to work. If we want to have a request where we intend to pass only those arguments that we intend to update, then we should use a PATCH request. Consider the following code:

```
def delete(self, id):
    product = Product.query.filter_by(id=id)
    product.delete()
    db.session.commit()
    return json.dumps({'response': 'Success'})
```

Last but not least, we have the DELETE request, which will simply delete the product that matches the `id` passed. Consider the following code:

```
api.add_resource(
    ProductApi,
    '/api/product',
    '/api/product/<int:id>',
    '/api/product/<int:id>/<int:page>'
)
```

The preceding code is the definition of all the possible routes our API can accommodate.

See also

▸ The API works in a manner similar to what was shown in the *Creating an extension-based REST interface* recipe

 An important facet of REST APIs is token-based authentication to allow only limited and authenticated users to be able to use and make calls to the API. I will urge you to explore this on your own. We covered the basics of user authentication in *Chapter 6, Authenticating in Flask*, which will serve as the base for this concept.

8

Admin Interface for Flask Apps

Every application needs an interface that provides special privileges to some users and can be used to maintain and upgrade the application resources. For example, we can have an interface in an e-commerce application; this interface will allow some special users to create categories, products, and so on. Some users might have permissions to handle other users who shop on the website and deal with their account information and so on. Similarly, there can be many cases where we will need to isolate an interface of our application from normal users.

In this chapter, we will cover the following recipes:

- ▶ Creating a simple CRUD interface
- ▶ Using the Flask-Admin extension
- ▶ Registering models with Flask-Admin
- ▶ Creating custom forms and actions
- ▶ WYSIWYG for textarea integration
- ▶ Creating user roles

Introduction

As opposed to the much popular Python-based web framework, Django, Flask does not provide an admin interface by default. Although this can be seen as a shortcoming by many, this gives the developers the flexibility to create the admin interface as per their requirements and have complete control over the application.

We can opt to write an admin interface for our application from scratch or use an extension of Flask, which does most of the work for us and gives us the option to customize the logic as needed. One very popular extension for creating admin interfaces in Flask is Flask-Admin (`https://pypi.python.org/pypi/Flask-Admin`), which is inspired by the Django admin but is implemented in a way that the developer has complete control over the look, feel, and functionality of the application. In this chapter, we will start with the creation of an admin interface on our own and then move onto using the Flask-Admin extension and fine-tuning it as needed.

Creating a simple CRUD interface

CRUD refers to **Create**, **Read**, **Update**, and **Delete**. A basic necessity of having an admin interface is to have the ability to create, modify, or delete the records/resources from the application as and when needed. We will create a simple admin interface that will allow the admin users to perform these operations on the records that other normal users generally can't.

Getting ready

We will start with our authentication application from the *Authenticating using the Flask-Login extension* recipe in *Chapter 6*, *Authenticating in Flask*, and add admin authentication and an interface for admins to the same, to allow only the admin users to create, update, and delete user records. Here, in this recipe, I will cover some specific parts that are needed to understand the concepts. For the complete application, refer to the code samples available with the book.

How to do it...

We will start with our models by adding a new field called `admin` to the `User` model in `models.py`. This field will help in identifying whether the user is an admin or not:

```
from wtforms import BooleanField

class User(db.Model):
    id = db.Column(db.Integer, primary_key=True)
    username = db.Column(db.String(60))
    pwdhash = db.Column(db.String())
    admin = db.Column(db.Boolean())

    def __init__(self, username, password, admin=False):
        self.username = username
        self.pwdhash = generate_password_hash(password)
```

```
        self.admin = admin

    def is_admin(self):
        return self.admin
```

The preceding method simply returns the value of the `admin` field. This can have a custom implementation as per your needs. Consider the following code:

```
class AdminUserCreateForm(Form):
    username = TextField('Username', [InputRequired()])
    password = PasswordField('Password', [InputRequired()])
    admin = BooleanField('Is Admin ?')



class AdminUserUpdateForm(Form):
    username = TextField('Username', [InputRequired()])
    admin = BooleanField('Is Admin ?')
```

Also, we created two forms that will be used by our admin views.

Now, we will modify our views in `views.py` to implement the admin interface:

```
from functools import wraps
from my_app.auth.models import AdminUserCreateForm,
AdminUserUpdateForm

def admin_login_required(func):
    @wraps(func)
    def decorated_view(*args, **kwargs):
        if not current_user.is_admin():
            return abort(403)
        return func(*args, **kwargs)
    return decorated_view
```

The preceding code is the `admin_login_required` decorator that works just like the `login_required` decorator. The difference is that it needs to be implemented along with `login_required`, and it checks if the currently logged-in user is an admin.

The following are all the handlers that we will need to create a simple admin interface. Note the usage of the `@admin_login_required` decorator. Everything else is pretty much standard as we learned in the previous chapters of this book, which focused on views and authentication handling:

```
@auth.route('/admin')
@login_required
@admin_login_required
```

```
def home_admin():
    return render_template('admin-home.html')

@auth.route('/admin/users-list')
@login_required
@admin_login_required
def users_list_admin():
    users = User.query.all()
    return render_template('users-list-admin.html', users=users)

@auth.route('/admin/create-user', methods=['GET', 'POST'])
@login_required
@admin_login_required
def user_create_admin():
    form = AdminUserCreateForm(request.form)

    if form.validate():
        username = form.username.data
        password = form.password.data
        admin = form.admin.data
        existing_username = User.query.filter_by
           (username=username).first()
        if existing_username:
            flash(
                'This username has been already taken. Try another
one.',
                'warning'
            )
            return render_template('register.html', form=form)
        user = User(username, password, admin)
        db.session.add(user)
        db.session.commit()
        flash('New User Created.', 'info')
        return redirect(url_for('auth.users_list_admin'))

    if form.errors:
        flash(form.errors, 'danger')

    return render_template('user-create-admin.html', form=form)
```

The preceding method allows admin users to create new users in the system. This works in a manner pretty similar to the `register()` method but allows the admins to set the `admin` flag on the users. Consider the following code:

```
@auth.route('/admin/update-user/<id>', methods=['GET', 'POST'])
@login_required
@admin_login_required
def user_update_admin(id):
    user = User.query.get(id)
    form = AdminUserUpdateForm(
        request.form,
        username=user.username,
        admin=user.admin
    )

    if form.validate():
        username = form.username.data
        admin = form.admin.data

        User.query.filter_by(id=id).update({
            'username': username,
            'admin': admin,
        })

        db.session.commit()
        flash('User Updated.', 'info')
        return redirect(url_for('auth.users_list_admin'))

    if form.errors:
        flash(form.errors, 'danger')

    return render_template('user-update-admin.html', form=form,
        user=user)
```

The preceding method allows the admin users to update the records of other users. However, as per best practices of writing web applications, we do not allow the admins to simply view and change the passwords of any user. In most cases, the provision to change passwords should rest with the user who owns the account. Admins, though, can have the provision to update the password in some cases, but still, it should never be possible for them to see the passwords set by the user earlier. This is the topic for discussion in the *Creating custom forms and actions* recipe. Consider the following code:

```
@auth.route('/admin/delete-user/<id>')
@login_required
@admin_login_required
```

```
def user_delete_admin(id):
    user = User.query.get(id)
    user.delete()

    db.session.commit()
    flash('User Deleted.')
    return redirect(url_for('auth.users_list_admin'))
```

The `user_delete_admin()` method should actually be implemented on a POST request. This is left to the readers to implement by themselves.

Followed by models and views, we will create some templates to complement them. It might have been evident to many of us from the code of the views itself that we need to add four new templates, namely, `admin-home.html`, `user-create-admin.html`, `user-update-admin.html`, and `users-list-admin.html`. How these work is shown in the next section. Readers should now be able to implement these templates by themselves, but for reference, the code is always available with the samples provided with the book.

How it works...

To start with, we added a menu item to the application; this provides a direct link to the admin home page, which will look like the following screenshot:

The menu item named Admin

A user must be logged in as admin to access this page and other admin-related pages. If a user is not logged in as admin, then the application will show an error, as shown in the following screenshot:

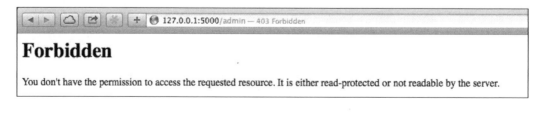

To a logged-in admin user, the admin home page will look as follows:

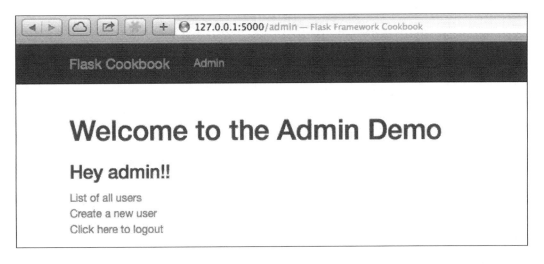

From here, the admin can see the list of users on a system or create a new user. The options to edit or delete the users will be available in the user list page itself.

 To set a user as the first admin, create a new user from the terminal using SQLAlchemy with the admin flag set to `True`.

Using the Flask-Admin extension

Flask-Admin is an available extension that helps in the creation of admin interfaces for our application in a simpler and faster way. All the subsequent recipes in this chapter will focus on using and extending this extension.

Getting ready

First, we need to install the Flask-Admin extension:

```
$ pip install Flask-Admin
```

We will extend our application from the first recipe and keep building over the same.

How to do it...

Adding a simple admin interface to any Flask application using the Flask-Admin extension is just a matter of a couple of statements.

We just need to add the following lines to our application's configuration:

```
from flask.ext.admin import Admin

app = Flask(__name__)

# Add any other application configuration

admin = Admin(app)
```

Just initializing an application with the `Admin` class from the Flask-Admin extension will put up a basic admin page, as shown in the following screenshot:

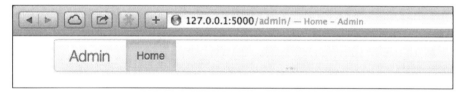

The admin page as created by Flask-Admin

Notice the URL in the screenshot, which is `http://127.0.0.1:5000/admin/`. We can also add our own views to it; this is as simple as adding a new class as a new view that inherits from the `BaseView` class:

```
from flask.ext.admin import BaseView, expose

class HelloView(BaseView):
    @expose('/')
    def index(self):
        return self.render('some-template.html')
```

After this, we will need to add this view to our `admin` object in the Flask configuration:

```
import my_app.auth.views as views

admin.add_view(views.HelloView(name='Hello'))
```

This will make the admin page look like the following screenshot:

One thing to notice here is that this page does not have any authentication or authorization logic implemented by default, and it will be accessible to all. The reason for this is that Flask-Admin does not make any assumptions about the authentication system in place. As we are using Flask-Login for our applications, we can add a method named `is_accessible()` to our `HelloView` class:

```
def is_accessible(self):
    return current_user.is_authenticated() and
        current_user.is_admin()
```

There's more...

After implementing the preceding code, there is still an admin view that won't be completely user protected and will be publicly available. This will be the admin home page. To make this available only to the admins, we have to inherit from `AdminIndexView` and implement `is_accessible()`:

```
from flask.ext.admin import AdminIndexView

class MyAdminIndexView(AdminIndexView):
    def is_accessible(self):
        return current_user.is_authenticated() and
            current_user.is_admin()
```

Then, just pass this view to the `admin` object in the application's configuration as `index_view`, and we are done:

```
admin = Admin(app, index_view=views.MyAdminIndexView())
```

This approach makes all our admin views accessible only to the admin users. We can also implement any permission or conditional access rules in `is_accessible()` as and when required.

Registering models with Flask-Admin

In the last recipe, we saw how to get started with the Flask-Admin extension to create admin interfaces/views to our application. In this recipe, we will see how to implement admin views for our existing models with the facilities to perform CRUD operations.

Getting ready

We will extend our application from the last recipe to include an admin interface for the User model.

How to do it...

Again, with Flask-Admin, registering a model with the admin interface is very easy. We just need to add a single line of code to get this:

```
from flask.ext.admin.contrib.sqla import ModelView

# Other admin configuration as shown in last recipe
admin.add_view(ModelView(views.User, db.session))
```

Here, in the first line, we imported ModelView from flask.ext.admin.contrib.sqla, which is provided by Flask-Admin to integrate SQLAlchemy models. This will create a new admin view for the User model; the view will look like the following screenshot:

Looking at the preceding screenshot, most of us will agree that showing the password hash to any user, be it admin or a normal user, does not make sense. Also, the default model-creation mechanism provided by Flask-Admin will fail for our User creation, because we have an __init__() method in our User model; this method expects values for the three fields, while the model-creation logic implemented in Flask-Admin is very generic and does not provide any value during model creation.

Now, we will customize the default behavior of Flask-Admin to something of our own where we fix the `User` creation mechanism and hide the password hash from the views:

```
class UserAdminView(ModelView):
    column_searchable_list = ('username',)
    column_sortable_list = ('username', 'admin')
    column_exclude_list = ('pwdhash',)
    form_excluded_columns = ('pwdhash',)
    form_edit_rules = ('username', 'admin')

    def is_accessible(self):
        return current_user.is_authenticated() and
            current_user.is_admin()
```

The preceding code shows some rules and settings that our admin view for `User` will follow. These are self-explanatory. A couple of them, `column_exclude_list` and `form_excluded_columns`, might seem a bit confusing. The former will exclude the columns mentioned from the admin view itself and refrain from using these columns in search, creation, and other CRUD operations. The latter will prevent the fields mentioned from being shown on the form for CRUD operations. Consider the following code:

```
def scaffold_form(self):
    form_class = super(UserAdminView, self).scaffold_form()
    form_class.password = PasswordField('Password')
    return form_class
```

The preceding method overrides the creation of the form from the model and adds a password field, which will be used in place of the password hash. Consider the following application:

```
def create_model(self, form):
    model = self.model(
        form.username.data, form.password.data,
            form.admin.data
    )
    form.populate_obj(model)
    self.session.add(model)
    self._on_model_change(form, model, True)
    self.session.commit()
```

The preceding method overrides the model-creation logic to suit our application.

To add this model to the `admin` object in the application config, we will write the following:

```
admin.add_view(views.UserAdminView(views.User, db.session))
```

Notice the `self._on_model_change(form, model, True)` statement. Here, `True`, the last parameter, signifies that the call is for the creation of a new record.

The admin interface for the `User` model will now look like the following screenshot:

```
◀ ▶  ☁ ☑ ✳ +  ⊕ 127.0.0.1:5000/admin/userview/ — User – Admin

    Admin    Home    User

    List (2)    Create    With selected ▾    Search

    ☐          Username                              Admin

    ☐  ✎ 🗑    admin                                 ✔

    ☐  ✎ 🗑    shalabh
```

We have a search box here, and no password hash is visible. There are changes to user creation and edit views too. I urge you to run the application to see for yourselves.

Creating custom forms and actions

In this recipe, we will create some custom forms using the forms provided by Flask-Admin. Also, we will create a custom action using the custom form.

Getting ready

In the last recipe, we saw that the edit form view for the `User` record update had no option to update the password for the user. The form looked like the following screenshot:

```
◀ ▶  ☁ ☑ ✳ +  ⊕ 127.0.0.1:5000/admin/userview/edit/?url=%2Fadmin%2Fuserview%2F&id=3 — User – Admin

    Admin    Home    User

    Username    shalabh

    Admin       ☑

                Submit    Save and Continue    Cancel
```

In this recipe, we will customize this form to allow administrators to update the password for any user.

How to do it...

The implementation of this feature will just require changes to `views.py`. First, we will start by importing `rules` from the Flask-Admin forms:

```
from flask.ext.admin.form import rules
```

In the last recipe, we had `form_edit_rules`, which had just two fields, that is, `username` and `admin` as a list. This denoted the fields that will be available for editing to the admin user on the `User` model update view.

Updating the password is not a simple affair of just adding one more field to the list of `form_edit_rules`, because we do not store cleartext passwords. We store password hashes instead, which cannot be edited directly by users. We need to input the password from the user and then convert it to a hash while storing. We will see how to do this in the following code:

```
form_edit_rules = (
    'username', 'admin',
    rules.Header('Reset Password'),
    'new_password', 'confirm'
)
form_create_rules = (
    'username', 'admin', 'notes', 'password'
)
```

The preceding piece of code signifies that we now have a header in our form; this header separates the password reset section from the rest of the section. Then, we will add two new fields, `new_password` and `confirm`, which will help us safely change the password:

```
def scaffold_form(self):
    form_class = super(UserAdminView, self).scaffold_form()
    form_class.password = PasswordField('Password')
    form_class.new_password = PasswordField('New Password')
    form_class.confirm = PasswordField('Confirm New Password')
    return form_class
```

This also calls for a change to the `scaffold_form()` method so that the two new fields become valid when the form renders.

Finally, we will implement the `update_model()` method, which is called when we try to update the record:

```
def update_model(self, form, model):
    form.populate_obj(model)
    if form.new_password.data:
        if form.new_password.data != form.confirm.data:
            flash('Passwords must match')
            return
        model.pwdhash = generate_password_hash
            (form.new_password.data)
    self.session.add(model)
    self._on_model_change(form, model, False)
    self.session.commit()
```

In the preceding code, we will first make sure that the password entered in both the fields is the same. If yes, we will proceed with resetting the password along with any other change.

Notice the `self._on_model_change(form, model, False)` statement. Here, `False`, as the last parameter, signifies that the call is not for the creation of a new record. This is also used in the last recipe, where we created the user. In that case, the last parameter was set to `True`.

How it works...

The user update form will now look like the following screenshot:

![User update form screenshot]

127.0.0.1:5000/admin/userview/edit/?url=%2Fadmin%2Fuserview%2F&id=3 — User – Admin

Admin Home User

Username   shalabh

Admin   ☑

Reset Password

New Password

Confirm New
Password

[Submit] [Save and Continue] [Cancel]

Here, if we enter the same password in both the password fields, the user password will be updated.

WYSIWYG for textarea integration

As users of websites, we all know that writing beautiful and formatted text using the normal textarea fields is a nightmare. There are plugins that make our life easier and turn simple textareas into **What you see is what you get** (**WYSIWYG**) editors. One such editor is **CKEditor**. It is open source, provides good flexibility, and has huge community support. Also, it is customizable and allows users to build add-ons as needed.

Getting ready

We start by adding a new textarea field to our `User` model for notes and then integrating this field with CKEditor to write formatted text. This will include the addition of a JavaScript library and a CSS class to a normal textarea field to convert it into a CKEditor-compatible textarea field.

How to do it...

First, we will add the `notes` field to the `User` model, which will then look as follows:

```python
class User(db.Model):
    id = db.Column(db.Integer, primary_key=True)
    username = db.Column(db.String(60))
    pwdhash = db.Column(db.String())
    admin = db.Column(db.Boolean())
    notes = db.Column(db.UnicodeText)

    def __init__(self, username, password, admin=False, notes=''):
        self.username = username
        self.pwdhash = generate_password_hash(password)
        self.admin = admin
        self.notes = notes
```

After this, we will create a custom `wtform` widget and field for a CKEditor textarea field:

```python
from wtforms import widgets, TextAreaField

class CKTextAreaWidget(widgets.TextArea):
    def __call__(self, field, **kwargs):
        kwargs.setdefault('class_', 'ckeditor')
        return super(CKTextAreaWidget, self).__call__(field,
            **kwargs)
```

In the custom widget in the preceding code, we added a `ckeditor` class to our `TextArea` widget. For more insights into the WTForm widgets, refer to the *Creating a custom widget* recipe in *Chapter 5, Webforms with WTForms*. Consider the following code:

```
class CKTextAreaField(TextAreaField):
    widget = CKTextAreaWidget()
```

In the custom field in the preceding code, we set the widget to `CKTextAreaWidget`, and when this field is rendered, the CSS class `ckeditor` will be added to it.

Next, we need to modify our form rules in the `UserAdminView` class, where we specify the template to be used for the create and edit forms. We will also override the normal `TextAreaField` with `CKTextAreaField` for `notes`:

```
form_overrides = dict(notes=CKTextAreaField)

create_template = 'edit.html'
edit_template = 'edit.html'
```

In the preceding code block, `form_overrides` enables the overriding of a normal textarea field with the CKEditor textarea field.

The last part in this recipe is the `templates/edit.html` template mentioned earlier:

```
{% extends 'admin/model/edit.html' %}

{% block tail %}
    {{ super() }}
    <script src="http://cdnjs.cloudflare.com/ajax/
        libs/ckeditor/4.0.1/ckeditor.js"></script>
{% endblock %}
```

Here, we extended the default `edit.html` file provided by Flask-Admin and added the CKEditor JS file so that our `ckeditor` class on `CKTextAreaField` works.

How it works...

After we have done all the changes, the user create form will look like the following screenshot. Notice the **Notes** field in particular.

Here, anything entered in the **Notes** field will be automatically formatted in HTML while saving and can be used anywhere later for display purposes.

See also

▶ This recipe is inspired from the gist by the author of Flask-Admin. The gist can be found at `https://gist.github.com/mrjoes/5189850`.

Creating user roles

Until now, we saw how a view that is accessible to a certain set of admin users can be created easily using the `is_accessible()` method. This can be extended to have different kinds of scenarios where specific users will be able to view specific views. There is another way of implementing user roles at a much more granular level in a model where the roles determine whether a user can perform all, some, or any of the CRUD operations.

Getting ready

In this recipe, we will see a basic way of creating user roles, where an admin user can only perform actions they are entitled to.

> Remember that this is just one way of implementing user roles. There are many better ways of doing this, but this one seems to be the best one to demonstrate the concept of creating user roles.
>
> One such method will be to create user groups and assign roles to the groups rather than individual users. Another method can be the complex policy-based user roles, which will include defining the roles according to complex business logic. This approach is usually employed by business systems such as ERP, CRM, and so on.

How to do it...

First, we will add a field named `roles` to the `User` model, which will then look as follows:

```
class User(db.Model):
    id = db.Column(db.Integer, primary_key=True)
    username = db.Column(db.String(60))
    pwdhash = db.Column(db.String())
    admin = db.Column(db.Boolean())
    notes = db.Column(db.UnicodeText)
    roles = db.Column(db.String(4))

    def __init__(self, username, password, admin=False, notes='',
      roles='R'):
        self.username = username
        self.pwdhash = generate_password_hash(password)
        self.admin = admin
        self.notes = notes
        self.roles = self.admin and self.roles or ''
```

Here, we added a new field, `roles`, which is a string field of length 4. We assumed that the only entries that are possible in this field are any combinations of C, R, U, and D. A user with the `roles` value as CRUD will have the permission to perform all the actions, while any missing permission will disallow the user from performing that action. Note that read permission is always implied to any admin user, whether specified or not.

Next, we need to make some changes to the `UserAdminView` class:

```
from flask.ext.admin.actions import ActionsMixin

class UserAdminView(ModelView, ActionsMixin):

    form_edit_rules = (
        'username', 'admin', 'roles', 'notes',
        rules.Header('Reset Password'),
        'new_password', 'confirm'
    )
    form_create_rules = (
        'username', 'admin', 'roles', 'notes', 'password'
    )
```

In the preceding code, we just added the `roles` field to our create and edit forms. We also inherited from a class called `ActionsMixin`. This is needed to handle the mass update actions such as mass deletion. Consider the following code:

```
def create_model(self, form):
    if 'C' not in current_user.roles:
        flash('You are not allowed to create users.',
            'warning')
        return
    model = self.model(
        form.username.data, form.password.data,
        form.admin.data,
        form.notes.data
    )
    form.populate_obj(model)
    self.session.add(model)
    self._on_model_change(form, model, True)
    self.session.commit()
```

In this method, we first checked if the `roles` field on `current_user` has the permission to create records (denoted by `C`). If not, we show an error message and return from the method. Consider the following code:

```
def update_model(self, form, model):
    if 'U' not in current_user.roles:
        flash('You are not allowed to edit users.', 'warning')
        return
    form.populate_obj(model)
    if form.new_password.data:
        if form.new_password.data != form.confirm.data:
            flash('Passwords must match')
```

```
                    return
                model.pwdhash = generate_password_hash
                    (form.new_password.data)
            self.session.add(model)
            self._on_model_change(form, model, False)
            self.session.commit()
```

In this method, we first checked if the `roles` field on `current_user` has the permission to update records (denoted by `U`). If not, show an error message and return from the method. Consider the following code:

```
    def delete_model(self, model):
        if 'D' not in current_user.roles:
            flash('You are not allowed to delete users.',
                'warning')
            return
        super(UserAdminView, self).delete_model(model)
```

Similarly, here we checked if `current_user` is allowed to delete records. Consider the following code:

```
    def is_action_allowed(self, name):
        if name == 'delete' and 'D' not in current_user.roles:
            flash('You are not allowed to delete users.',
                'warning')
            return False
        return True
```

In the preceding method, we checked if the action is `delete` and if `current_user` is allowed to delete. If not, then flash the error message and return a `False` value. This method can be extended to handle any custom-written actions too.

How it works...

This recipe works in a manner very similar to how our application has been working until now, except the fact that now, users with designated roles will be able to perform specified operations. Otherwise, error messages will be displayed.

The user list will now look like the following screenshot:

	Username	Admin	Roles
List (2) Create Search			
✏ 🗑	admin	✔	CRUD
✏ 🗑	shalabh	✔	U

To test the rest of the functionality, such as creating new users (both normal and admin), deleting users, updating user records, and so on, I urge you to try it for yourselves.

9

Internationalization and Localization

Web applications usually are not limited to one geographical region or to serving people from one linguistic domain. For example, a web application intended for users in Europe will be expected to support other European languages such as German, French, Italian, Spanish, and so on, apart from English. This chapter will cover the basics of how to enable support for multiple languages in a Flask application.

In this chapter, we will cover the following recipes:

- ▸ Adding a new language
- ▸ Lazy evaluation and the gettext/ngettext functions
- ▸ Global language-switching action

Introduction

Adding support for a second language in any web application is a tricky affair. It increases a bit of overhead every time some change is made to the application, and this increases with the number of languages. There can be a number of things that need to be taken care of, apart from just changing the text as per the language. Some of the major ones are currency, number, time and date formatting, and so on.

Flask-Babel, an extension that adds i18n and l10n support to any Flask application, provides some tools and techniques to make this process simpler and easy to implement.

 i18n stands for internationalization, and similarly, l10n stands for localization.

In this chapter, we will be using this extension extensively to understand the concepts mentioned.

Adding a new language

By default, English is the language for applications built in Flask (and almost all web frameworks). We will add a second language to our application and add some translations for the display strings used in the application. The language displayed to the user will vary depending on the current language set in the browser.

Getting ready

We will start with the installation of the Flask-Babel extension:

```
$ pip install Flask-Babel
```

This extension uses **Babel**, **pytz**, and **speaklater** to add i18n and l10n support to the application.

We will use our catalog application from *Chapter 5, Webforms with WTForms*.

How to do it...

First, we will start with the configuration part by creating an instance of the `Babel` class using the `app` object. We will also specify what languages will be available here. French is added as the second language:

```python
from flask.ext.babel import Babel

ALLOWED_LANGUAGES = {
    'en': 'English',
    'fr': 'French',
}
babel = Babel(app)
```

Here, we used en and fr as the language codes. These refer to English (standard) and French (standard), respectively. If we intend to support multiple languages that are from the same standard language origin but differ on the basis of regions such as English (US) and English (GB), then we should use codes such as en-us and en-gb.

Next, we will create a file in the application folder called babel.cfg. The path of this file will be flask_catalog/my_app/babel.cfg, and it will have the following content:

```
[python: catalog/**.py]
[jinja2: templates/**.html]
extensions=jinja2.ext.autoescape,jinja2.ext.with_
```

Here, the first two lines tell Babel about the file name patterns that are to be searched for marked translatable text. The third one loads some extensions that make this searching of text in the files possible.

The locale of the application depends on the output of the method that is decorated with the @babel.localeselector decorator. Add the following method to the views file, that is, views.py:

```
from my_app import babel, ALLOWED_LANGUAGES

@babel.localeselector
def get_locale():
    return request.accept_languages.best_match(ALLOWED_LANGUAGES.
keys())
```

The preceding method gets the Accept-Languages header from the request and finds the language that best matches the languages we allow.

It is pretty easy to change the language preferences in the browser. However, in any case, if you do not want to mess with the language preferences of the browser, simply return the expected language code from the get_locale() method.

Next, we will mark some text that is intended to be translated as per language mentioned. Let's start with the first text we see when we start our application, that is, in home.html:

```
{% block container %}
<h1>{{ _('Welcome to the Catalog Home') }}</h1>
  <a href="{{ url_for('products') }}" id="catalog_link">
  {{ _('Click here to see the catalog ') }}
  </a>
{% endblock %}
```

Here, _ is a shortcut for the `gettext` function provided by Babel to translate strings.

After this, we need to run the following commands so that the marked text is actually available as translated text in our template when it is rendered in the browser:

```
$ pybabel extract -F my_app/babel.cfg -o my_app/messages.pot
my_app
```

The preceding command traverses through the contents of the files; this command matches the patterns in `babel.cfg` and picks out the texts that have been marked as translatable. All these texts are placed in the `my_app/messages.pot` file. Consider the following command:

```
$ pybabel init -i my_app/messages.pot -d my_app/translations -l fr
```

The preceding `init` command creates a `.po` file, which will hold the translations for the texts to be translated. This file is created in the specified folder, `my_app/translations` as `fr/LC_MESSAGES/messages.po`. As we add more languages, more folders will be added.

Now, we need to add translations to the `messages.po` file. This can be manually done, or we can use GUI tools such as Poedit (`http://poedit.net/`). Using this tool, the translations will look like the following screenshot:

Source text	Translation — French
Name	Nom
Price	Prix
Category	Catégorie
Company	Entreprise
Product Image	Image du produit
Welcome to the Catalog Home	Bienvenue sur le catalogue Accueil
Click here to see the catalog	Cliquez ici pour voir le catalogue

Manual editing of `messages.po` will look like the following code. Only one message translation is shown for demonstration:

```
#: my_app/templates/home.html:6
msgid "Click here to see the catalog "
msgstr "Cliquez ici pour voir le catalogue "
```

Save the `messages.po` file after the translations have been put in and run the following command:

```
$ pybabel compile -d my_app/translations
```

This will create a `messages.mo` file next to the `message.po` file, which will be used by the application to render the translated text.

Sometimes, the messages do not get compiled after running the preceding command. This is because the messages might be marked as fuzzy (starting with a #). These need to be looked at by a human and the # sign has to be removed if the message is OK to be updated by the compiler. To bypass this check, add a -f flag to the preceding `compile` command as it will force everything to get compiled.

How it works...

If we run the application with French set as the primary language in the browser, the home page will look like the following screenshot:

Flask Cookbook

Bienvenue sur le catalogue Accueil

Cliquez ici pour voir le catalogue 10

If the primary language is set to something other than French, then the content will be shown in English, which is the default language.

My browser language settings currently look like the ones shown in the following screenshot:

Languages	✕

Add languages and drag to order them based on your preference. Learn more

Languages	**French – français**
French ✕	☐ Offer to translate pages in this language
English (United States)	
English	
Portuguese	
Portuguese (Brazil)	

There's more...

Next time, if we need to update the translations in our `messages.po` file, we do not need to call the `init` command again. Instead, we can run an `update` command, which is as follows:

```
$ pybabel update -i my_app/messages.pot -d my_app/translations
```

After this, run the `compile` command as usual.

 It is often desired to change the language of a website based on the user IP and location (determined from the IP). This is regarded as an inferior way of handling localization as compared to the use of the Accept-Language header, as we did in our application.

See also

▶ The *Global language-switching action* recipe to allow the user to change the language directly from the application rather than doing it at the browser level.

▶ An important aspect of multiple languages is to be able to format the date, time, and currency accordingly. Babel handles this also pretty neatly. I urge you to try your hands at this by yourself. Refer to the Babel documentation available at `http://babel.pocoo.org/docs/` for this.

Lazy evaluation and the gettext/ngettext functions

Lazy evaluation is an evaluation strategy that delays the evaluation of an expression until its value is needed, that is, it is a call-by-need mechanism. In our application, there can be several instances of texts that are evaluated later while rendering the template. It usually happens when we have texts that are marked as translatable outside the request context, so we defer the evaluation of these until they are actually needed.

Getting ready

Let's start with the application from the previous recipe. Now, we want the labels in the product- and category-creation forms to show the translated values.

How to do it...

To mark all the field labels in the product and category forms as translatable, we will make the following changes to `models.py`:

```python
from flask.ext.babel import _

class NameForm(Form):
    name = TextField(_('Name'), validators=[InputRequired()])

class ProductForm(NameForm):
    price = DecimalField(_('Price'), validators=[
        InputRequired(), NumberRange(min=Decimal('0.0'))
    ])
    category = CategoryField(
        _('Category'), validators=[InputRequired()], coerce=int
    )
    image = FileField(_('Product Image'))

class CategoryForm(NameForm):
    name = TextField(_('Name'), validators=[
        InputRequired(), check_duplicate_category()
    ])
```

Notice that all the field labels are enclosed within `_()` to be marked for translation.

Now, run the pybabel `extract` and `update` commands to update the `messages.po` file, and then fill in the relevant translations and run the `compile` command. Refer to the previous recipe, *Adding a new language*, for details.

Now, open the product-creation page using the link `http://127.0.0.1:5000/product-create`. However, does it work as expected? No! As most of us would have guessed by now, the reason for this behavior is that this text is marked for translation outside the request context.

To make this work, we just need to modify the `import` statement to the following:

```python
from flask.ext.babel import lazy_gettext as _
```

Now, we have more text to translate. Let's say we want to translate the product-creation flash message content, which looks as follows:

```python
flash('The product %s has been created' % name)
```

To mark it as translatable, we cannot just simply wrap the whole thing inside _() or gettext(). The gettext() function supports placeholders, which can be used as %(name)s. Using this, the preceding code will become something like:

```
flash(_('The product %(name)s has been created', name=name))
```

The resulting translated text for this will be like Le produit %(name)s a été créé.

There might be cases where we need to manage the translations based on the number of items, that is, singular or plural names. This is handled by the ngettext() method. Let's take an example where we want to show the number of pages in our products.html template. For this, we need to add the following:

```
{{ ngettext('%(num)d page', '%(num)d pages', products.pages) }}
```

Here, the template will render page if there is only page and pages if there is more than one page.

It is interesting to note how this translation looks in the messages.po file:

```
#: my_app/templates/products.html:20
#, python-format
msgid "%(num)d page"
msgid_plural "%(num)d pages"
msgstr[0] "%(num)d page"
msgstr[1] "%(num)d pages"
```

The preceding code makes the concept clear.

Global language-switching action

In the previous recipes, we saw that the languages change on the basis of the current language preferences in the browser. However, now, we want a mechanism where we can switch the language to be used irrespective of the language in the browser. For this, we need to handle the language at the application level.

Getting ready

We start by modifying the application from the last recipe, *Lazy evaluation and the gettext/ngettext functions*, to accommodate the changes to enable language switching. We will add an extra URL part to all our routes to add the current language. We can just change this language in the URL to switch between languages.

How to do it...

The first change that we need to do is modify all our URL rules to accommodate an extra URL part. So `@app.route('/')` will become `@app.route('/<lang>/')`, and `@app.route('/home')` will become `@app.route('/<lang>/home')`. Similarly, `@app.route('/product-search/<int:page>')` will become `@app.route('/<lang>/product-search/<int:page>')`. The same needs to be done for all the URL rules.

Now, we need to add a function that will add the language passed in the URL to the global proxy object g:

```
@app.before_request
def before():
    if request.view_args and 'lang' in request.view_args:
        g.current_lang = request.view_args['lang']
        request.view_args.pop('lang')
```

This method will run before each request and add the current language to g.

However, this will mean that all the `url_for()` calls in the application need to be modified to have an extra parameter called `lang` to be passed. Fortunately, there is an easy way out of this, which is as follows:

```
from flask import url_for as flask_url_for

@app.context_processor
def inject_url_for():
    return {
        'url_for': lambda endpoint, **kwargs: flask_url_for(
            endpoint, lang=g.current_lang, **kwargs
        )
    }

url_for = inject_url_for()['url_for']
```

In the preceding code, we first imported `url_for` from `flask` as `flask_url_for`. Then, we updated the application context processor to have the `url_for()` function, which is a modified version of `url_for()` provided by Flask to have `lang` as an extra parameter.

How it works...

Now, run the application as it is and you will notice that all the URLs will have a language part. The following two screenshots explain how the rendered templates will look.

On opening `http://127.0.0.1:5000/en/home`, we see the following:

The home page with English as the language

Now, just change the URL to `http://127.0.0.1:5000/fr/home`, and the home page will look like the following screenshot:

Bienvenue sur le catalogue Accueil

Cliquez ici pour voir le catalogue

The home page with French as the language

See also

> ▶ The recipe, *Adding a new language*, to handle localization based on the language set in the browser (which is, by default, picked up from the language set at the OS level)

10
Debugging, Error Handling, and Testing

Until now, in this book, we have concentrated on developing applications and adding features to them one at a time. It is very important to know how robust our application is and keep track of how the application has been working and performing. This, in turn, gives rise to the need of being informed when something goes wrong in the application. It is normal to miss out on certain edge cases while developing an application, and usually, even the test cases miss them out. It will be great to know these edge cases whenever they occur so that they can be handled accordingly.

Testing in itself is a very huge topic, and has several books attributed to it. Here, we will try to understand the basics of testing with Flask.

In this chapter, we will cover the following recipes:

- ▶ Setting up basic file logging
- ▶ Sending e-mails on the occurrence of errors
- ▶ Using Sentry to monitor exceptions
- ▶ Debugging with pdb
- ▶ Creating our first simple test
- ▶ Writing more tests for views and logic
- ▶ Nose library integration
- ▶ Using mocking to avoid real API access
- ▶ Determining test coverage
- ▶ Using profiling to find bottlenecks

Introduction

Effective logging and the ability to debug quickly are some of the deciding factors to choose a framework for application development. The better the logging and debugging support from the framework, the quicker the process of application development and the easier the maintenance in future. It helps developers quickly find out the issues in the application, and many times, logging points out the issues even before they are identified by the end users. Effective error handling plays an important role in end user satisfaction and eases the pain of debugging at the developers' end. Even if the code is perfect, the application is bound to throw errors at times. Why? The answer is simple: the code might be perfect, but the world in which it works is not. There can be innumerable issues that can occur, and as developers, we always want to know the reason behind any anomaly. Writing test cases along with the application is one of the most important pillars of software writing.

Python's inbuilt logging system works pretty well with Flask. We will work with this logging system in this chapter before moving on to an awesome service called **Sentry**, which eases the pain of debugging and error logging to a huge extent.

As we have already talked about the importance of testing for application development, we will now see how to write test cases for a Flask application. We will also see how we can measure code coverage and profile our application to tackle any bottlenecks.

Setting up basic file logging

By default, Flask will not log anything for us anywhere, except for the errors with their stack traces, which are sent to the logger (we will see more of this in the remaining part of the chapter). This creates a lot of stack traces when we run the application in the development mode using `run.py`, but in production systems, we don't have this luxury. Thankfully, the logging library provides a whole lot of log handlers, which can be used as per our requirements.

Getting ready

We will start with our catalog application and add some basic logging to it using `FileHandler`, which logs messages to a specified file on the filesystem. We will start with a basic log format and then see how to format the log messages to be more informative.

How to do it...

As always, the first change is made to the `__init__.py` file, which serves as the application's configuration file:

```
app.config['LOG_FILE'] = 'application.log'

if not app.debug:
```

```
import logging
from logging import FileHandler
file_handler = FileHandler(app.config['LOG_FILE'])
file_handler.setLevel(logging.INFO)
app.logger.addHandler(file_handler)
```

Here, we added a configuration parameter to specify the logfile's location. This takes the relative path from the application folder, unless an absolute path is explicitly specified. Next, we will check whether the application is not already in the mode, and then, we will add a handler logging to a file with the logging level as `INFO`. `DEBUG` is the lowest logging level and will log everything at any level. For more details, refer to the logging library documentation (link available in the *See also* section).

After this, we just need to add loggers to our application wherever they are needed, and our application will start logging to the deputed file. Let's add a couple of loggers for demonstration to `views.py`:

```
@catalog.route('/')
@catalog.route('/<lang>/')
@catalog.route('/<lang>/home')
@template_or_json('home.html')
def home():
    products = Product.query.all()
    app.logger.info(
        'Home page with total of %d products' % len(products)
    )
    return {'count': len(products)}


@catalog.route('/<lang>/product/<id>')
def product(id):
    product = Product.query.filter_by(id=id).first()
    if not product:
        app.logger.warning('Requested product not found.')
        abort(404)
    return render_template('product.html', product=product)
```

In the preceding code, we have loggers to a couple of our view handlers. Notice that the first of the loggers in `home()` is of the `info` level and the other in `product()` is `warning`. If we set our log level in `__init__.py` as `INFO`, then both will be logged, and if we set the level as `WARNING`, then only the warning logger will be logged.

How it works...

The preceding piece of code will create a file called `application.log` at the root application folder. The logger statements as specified will be logged to this file and will look something like the following snippet, depending on the handler called; the first one being from `home` and the second from requesting a product that does not exist:

```
Home page with total of 1 products
Requested product not found.
```

There's more...

The information logged does not help much. It will be great to know when the issue was logged, with what level, which file caused the issue at what line number, and so on. This can be achieved using advanced logging formats. For this, we need to add a couple of statements to the configuration file, that is, `__init__.py`:

```python
if not app.debug:
    import logging
    from logging import FileHandler, Formatter
    file_handler = FileHandler(app.config['LOG_FILE'])
    file_handler.setLevel(logging.WARNING)
    app.logger.addHandler(file_handler)
    file_handler.setFormatter(Formatter(
        '%(asctime)s %(levelname)s: %(message)s '
        '[in %(pathname)s:%(lineno)d]'
    ))
```

In the preceding code, we added a formatter to `file_handler`, which will log the time, log level, message, file path, and line number. After this, the logged message will look as follows:

```
2014-08-02 15:18:21,154 WARNING: Requested product not found. [in /Users/
shalabhaggarwal/workspace/mydev/flask_catalog_testing_lgging/my_app/
catalog/views.py:50]
```

See also

▶ Read through Python's logging library documentation about handlers at
   `https://docs.python.org/dev/library/logging.handlers.html`
   to know more about logging handlers

Sending e-mails on the occurrence of errors

It is a good idea to receive errors when something unexpected happens with the application. Setting this up is pretty easy and adds a lot of convenience to the process of error handling.

Getting ready

We will take the application from the last recipe and add `mail_handler` to it to make our application send e-mails when an error occurs. Also, we will demonstrate how to set up these e-mails using Gmail as the SMTP server.

How to do it...

We will first add the handler to our configuration in `__init__.py`. This is similar to how we added `file_handler` in the last recipe:

```python
RECIPIENTS = ['some_receiver@gmail.com']

if not app.debug:
    import logging
    from logging import FileHandler, Formatter
    from logging.handlers import SMTPHandler
    file_handler = FileHandler(app.config['LOG_FILE'])
    file_handler.setLevel(logging.INFO)
    app.logger.addHandler(file_handler)
    mail_handler = SMTPHandler(
        ("smtp.gmail.com", 587), 'sender@gmail.com', RECIPIENTS,
        'Error occurred in your application',
        ('sender@gmail.com', 'some_gmail_password'), secure=())
    mail_handler.setLevel(logging.ERROR)
    app.logger.addHandler(mail_handler)
    for handler in [file_handler, mail_handler]:
        handler.setFormatter(Formatter(
            '%(asctime)s %(levelname)s: %(message)s '
            '[in %(pathname)s:%(lineno)d]'
        ))
```

Here, we have a list of e-mail addresses to which the error notification e-mail will be sent. Also note that we have set the log level to ERROR in the case of `mail_handler`. This is because e-mails will be necessary only in the case of crucial and important matters.

For more details on the configuration of `SMTPHandler`, refer to the documentation.

> Always make sure that you turn the `debug` flag off in `run.py` to enable the application to log and send e-mails for internal application errors (error 500).

How it works...

To cause an internal application error, just misspell a keyword in any of your handlers. You will receive an e-mail in your mailbox, with the formatting as set in the configuration and a complete stack trace for your reference.

There's more...

We might also want to log all the errors when a page is not found (error 404). For this, we can just tweak the `errorhandler` method a bit:

```
@app.errorhandler(404)
def page_not_found(e):
    app.logger.error(e)
    return render_template('404.html'), 404
```

Using Sentry to monitor exceptions

Sentry is a tool that eases the process of monitoring exceptions and also provides insights into the errors that the users of the application face while using it. It is highly possible that there are errors in logfiles that get missed out by the human eye. Sentry categorizes the errors under different categories and keeps a count of the recurrence of errors. This helps in understanding the severity of the errors on multiple criteria and helps us to handle them accordingly. It has a nice GUI that facilitates all of these features.

Getting ready

We will start with the Sentry installation and configuration procedure. There are multiple ways of installing and configuring Sentry as per our needs. Sentry also provides a SaaS-based hosted solution where you can just skip the installation part discussed ahead and move on directly to integration. You can get Sentry from `https://www.getsentry.com`.

Here, we will discuss a very basic version of the Sentry installation and configuration procedure, and the rest can be taken up by you when your level of familiarity with Sentry increases. We will use PostgreSQL as the database for Sentry, as it is highly recommended by the Sentry team itself, so we will run the following command:

```
$ pip install sentry[postgres]
```

Sentry is a server application that will need a client library to access it. The recommended client is **Raven**, which can be simply installed for a Flask-based setup by running the following command:

```
$ pip install raven[flask]
```

There is another library named **blinker** that is also needed. It is used to handle signals from the Flask application (this is out of the scope of this book, but you can read more about it at https://pypi.python.org/pypi/blinker). It can be installed using the following command:

```
$ pip install blinker
```

How to do it...

Following the installations, we need to do some configurations for the Sentry server. First, initialize the config file in a path of your choice. I prefer to initialize it inside a folder named etc in the current virtualenv. This can be done using the following command:

```
$ sentry init etc/sentry.conf.py
```

Then, the basic configuration will look something like the following code:

```
from sentry.conf.server import *

DATABASES = {
    'default': {
        'ENGINE': 'django.db.backends.postgresql_psycopg2',
        'NAME': 'sentry', # Name of the postgres database
        'USER': 'postgres', # Name of postgres user
        'PASSWORD': '',
        'HOST': '',
        'PORT': '',
        'OPTIONS': {
            'autocommit': True,
        }
    }
}
SENTRY_URL_PREFIX = 'http://localhost:9000'

SENTRY_WEB_HOST = '0.0.0.0'
SENTRY_WEB_PORT = 9000
SENTRY_WEB_OPTIONS = {
    'workers': 3,   # the number of gunicorn workers
    'limit_request_line': 0,   # required for raven-js
    'secure_scheme_headers': {'X-FORWARDED-PROTO': 'https'},
}
```

We can also configure the mail server details so that Sentry can send e-mails when errors are encountered and effectively take the overhead from the logging library, as we did in the last recipe. More about this can be read at `http://sentry.readthedocs.org/en/latest/ quickstart/index.html#configure-outbound-mail`.

Now, in `postgres`, we need to create the database that we used in our Sentry configuration and upgrade the initial schema:

```
$ createdb -E utf-8 sentry
$ sentry --config=etc/sentry.conf.py upgrade
```

The upgrade process will create a default superuser. If it does not, do so yourself by running the following commands:

```
$ sentry --config=etc/sentry.conf.py createsuperuser
Username: sentry
Email address: someuser@example.com
Password:
Password (again):
Superuser created successfully.
$ sentry --config=etc/sentry.conf.py repair –owner=sentry
```

In the last command, `sentry` is the username that was chosen while creating the superuser.

Now, just start the Sentry server by running the following command:

```
$ sentry --config=etc/sentry.conf.py start
```

By default, Sentry runs on port 9000 and can be accessed at `http://localhost:9000/`.

Next, we need to create a team in Sentry using the GUI and then create a project to record our application's error logs. After you log in to Sentry using the superuser credentials, you will see a button, as shown in the following screenshot:

Create a team and project as the forms ask for. The project form will look like the following screenshot:

After this, a screen like the one in the following screenshot will be shown. The details here will be used in our Flask application's configuration.

Now, simply copy the details highlighted in the preceding screenshot and place them in the Flask configuration file. This will enable the logging of any uncaught errors to Sentry.

How it works...

An error logged in Sentry will look like the following screenshot:

It is also possible to log messages and user-defined exceptions in Sentry. I leave this to you to figure out by yourself.

Debugging with pdb

Most of the Python developers reading this book might already be aware of the usage of **pdb**, that is, the Python debugger. For those who are not aware of it, pdb is an interactive source code debugger for Python programs. We can set breakpoints wherever needed, debug using single-stepping at the source line level, and inspect the stack frames.

Many new developers might be of the opinion that the job of a debugger can be handled using a logger, but debuggers provide a much deeper insight into the flow of control and preserve the state at each step, and hence, save a lot of development time.

Getting ready

We will use Python's built-in pdb module for this recipe and use it in our application from the last recipe.

How to do it...

Using pdb is pretty simple in most cases. We just need to insert the following statement wherever we want to insert a breakpoint to inspect a certain block of code:

```
import pdb; pdb.set_trace()
```

This will trigger the application to break execution at this point, and then, we can step through the stack frames one by one using the debugger commands.

So, let's insert this statement in one of our methods, say, the handler for products:

```
def products(page=1):
    products = Product.query.paginate(page, 10)
    import pdb; pdb.set_trace()
    return render_template('products.html', products=products)
```

Whenever the control comes to this line, the debugger prompt will fire up; this will look as follows:

```
-> return render_template('products.html', products=product)

(Pdb) u

> /Users/shalabhaggarwal/workspace/flask_heroku/lib/python2.7/site-
packages/Flask-0.10.1-py2.7.egg/flask/app.py(1461)dispatch_request()

-> return self.view_functions[rule.endpoint](**req.view_args)

(Pdb) u

> /Users/shalabhaggarwal/workspace/flask_heroku/lib/python2.7/site-
packages/Flask-0.10.1-py2.7.egg/flask/app.py(1475)full_dispatch_request()

-> rv = self.dispatch_request()

(Pdb) u

> /Users/shalabhaggarwal/workspace/flask_heroku/lib/python2.7/site-
packages/Flask-0.10.1-py2.7.egg/flask/app.py(1817)wsgi_app()

-> response = self.full_dispatch_request()
```

Notice the u written against (Pdb). This signifies that I am moving the current frame one level up in the stack trace. All the variables, parameters, and properties used in that statement will be available in the same context to help figure out the issue or just understand the flow of code.

See also

> ▶ Check out the pdb module documentation at `https://docs.python.org/2/library/pdb.html#debugger-commands` to get hold of the various debugger commands

Creating our first simple test

Testing is one of the pillars of any software during development, and later during maintenance and expansion too. Especially in the case of web applications where the application will handle high traffic and be scrutinized by a large number of end users at all times, testing becomes pretty important, as the user feedback determines the fate of the application. In this recipe, we will see how to start with test writing and also see more complex tests in the recipes to follow.

Getting ready

We will start with the creation of a new test file named `app_tests.py` at the root application level, that is, alongside the `my_app` folder.

The `unittest2` Python library also needs to be installed using the following command:

```
$ pip install unittest2
```

How to do it...

To start with, the contents of the `app_tests.py` test file will be as follows:

```python
import os
from my_app import app, db
import unittest2 as unittest
import tempfile
```

The preceding code describes the imports needed for this test suite. We will use `unittest2` for our testing (install it using `pip` if not installed already). A `tempfile` is needed to create SQLite databases on the fly.

All the test cases need to subclass from `unitest.TestCase`:

```python
class CatalogTestCase(unittest.TestCase):

    def setUp(self):
        self.test_db_file = tempfile.mkstemp()[1]
        app.config['SQLALCHEMY_DATABASE_URI'] = 'sqlite:///' +
            self.test_db_file
        app.config['TESTING'] = True
        self.app = app.test_client()
        db.create_all()
```

The preceding method is run before each test is run and creates a new test client. A test is represented by the methods in this class that start with the `test_` prefix. Here, we set a database name in the app configuration, which is a timestamp that will always be unique. We also set the `TESTING` flag to `True`, which disables error catching to enable better testing. Finally, we ran the `create_all()` method on `db` to create all the tables from our application in the test database created. Consider the following code:

```python
    def tearDown(self):
        os.remove(self.test_db_file)
```

The preceding method is called after each test is run. Here, we will remove the current database file and use a fresh database file for each test. Consider the following code:

```
def test_home(self):
    rv = self.app.get('/')
    self.assertEqual(rv.status_code, 200)
```

The preceding code is our first test where we sent an HTTP GET request to our application at the / URL and tested the response for the status code, which should be 200; this represents a successful GET response.

```
if __name__ == '__main__':
    unittest.main()
```

How it works...

To run the test file, just execute the following command in the terminal:

```
$ python app_tests.py
```

The following screenshot shows the output that signifies the outcome of the tests:

See also

▶ Check out the next recipe, *Writing more tests for views and logic*, to see more on how to write complex tests

Writing more tests for views and logic

In the last recipe, we got started with writing tests for our Flask application. In this recipe, we will build upon the same test file and add more tests for our application; these tests will cover testing the views for behavior and logic.

Getting ready

We will build upon the test file named app_tests.py created in the last recipe.

How to do it...

Before we write any tests, we need to add a small bit of configuration to `setUp()` to disable the CSRF tokens, as they are not generated by default for test environments:

```
app.config['WTF_CSRF_ENABLED'] = False
```

The following are some tests that are created as a part of this recipe. Each test will be described as we go further:

```
def test_products(self):
    "Test Products list page"
    rv = self.app.get('/en/products')
    self.assertEqual(rv.status_code, 200)
    self.assertTrue('No Previous Page' in rv.data)
    self.assertTrue('No Next Page' in rv.data)
```

The preceding test sends a GET request to `/products` and asserts that the status code of the response is 200. It also asserts that there is no previous page and no next page (rendered as a part of template logic). Consider the following code:

```
def test_create_category(self):
    "Test creation of new category"
    rv = self.app.get('/en/category-create')
    self.assertEqual(rv.status_code, 200)

    rv = self.app.post('/en/category-create')
    self.assertEqual(rv.status_code, 200)
    self.assertTrue('This field is required.' in rv.data)

    rv = self.app.get('/en/categories')
    self.assertEqual(rv.status_code, 404)
    self.assertFalse('Phones' in rv.data)

    rv = self.app.post('/en/category-create', data={
        'name': 'Phones',
    })
    self.assertEqual(rv.status_code, 302)

    rv = self.app.get('/en/categories')
    self.assertEqual(rv.status_code, 200)
    self.assertTrue('Phones' in rv.data)

    rv = self.app.get('/en/category/1')
    self.assertEqual(rv.status_code, 200)
    self.assertTrue('Phones' in rv.data)
```

The preceding test creates a category and asserts for corresponding status messages. When a category is successfully created, we will redirect to the newly created category page, and hence, the status code will be 302. Consider the following code:

```
def test_create_product(self):
    "Test creation of new product"
    rv = self.app.get('/en/product-create')
    self.assertEqual(rv.status_code, 200)

    rv = self.app.post('/en/product-create')
    self.assertEqual(rv.status_code, 200)
    self.assertTrue('This field is required.' in rv.data)

    # Create a category to be used in product creation
    rv = self.app.post('/en/category-create', data={
        'name': 'Phones',
    })
    self.assertEqual(rv.status_code, 302)

    rv = self.app.post('/en/product-create', data={
        'name': 'iPhone 5',
        'price': 549.49,
        'company': 'Apple',
        'category': 1
    })
    self.assertEqual(rv.status_code, 302)

    rv = self.app.get('/en/products')
    self.assertEqual(rv.status_code, 200)
    self.assertTrue('iPhone 5' in rv.data)
```

The preceding test creates a product and asserts for corresponding status messages on each call.

As part of this test, we identified a small improvement in our `create_product()` method. What looked like `image = request.files['image']` earlier has now been replaced by `image = request.files` and `request.files['image']`. This is because in the case of an HTML form, we had an empty `request.files['image']` parameter, but in this case, we don't.

Consider the following code:

```python
def test_search_product(self):
    "Test searching product"
    # Create a category to be used in product creation
    rv = self.app.post('/en/category-create', data={
        'name': 'Phones',
    })
    self.assertEqual(rv.status_code, 302)

    # Create a product
    rv = self.app.post('/en/product-create', data={
        'name': 'iPhone 5',
        'price': 549.49,
        'company': 'Apple',
        'category': 1
    })
    self.assertEqual(rv.status_code, 302)

    # Create another product
    rv = self.app.post('/en/product-create', data={
        'name': 'Galaxy S5',
        'price': 549.49,
        'company': 'Samsung',
        'category': 1
    })
    self.assertEqual(rv.status_code, 302)

    self.app.get('/')

    rv = self.app.get('/en/product-search?name=iPhone')
    self.assertEqual(rv.status_code, 200)
    self.assertTrue('iPhone 5' in rv.data)
    self.assertFalse('Galaxy S5' in rv.data)

    rv = self.app.get('/en/product-search?name=iPhone 6')
    self.assertEqual(rv.status_code, 200)
    self.assertFalse('iPhone 6' in rv.data)
```

The preceding test first creates a category and two products. Then, it searches for one product and makes sure that only the searched product is returned in the result.

How it works...

To run the test file, just execute the following command in the terminal:

```
$ python app_tests.py -v
test_create_category (__main__.CatalogTestCase)
Test creation of new category ... ok
test_create_product (__main__.CatalogTestCase)
Test creation of new product ... ok
test_home (__main__.CatalogTestCase)
Test home page ... ok
test_products (__main__.CatalogTestCase)
Test Products list page ... ok
test_search_product (__main__.CatalogTestCase)
Test searching product ... ok
----------------------------------------------------------------------
Ran 5 tests in 0.189s

OK
```

What follows the command is the output that signifies the outcome of tests.

Nose library integration

Nose is a library that makes testing easier and much more fun. It provides a whole lot of tools to enhance our tests. Although Nose can be used for multiple purposes, the most important usage remains that of a test collector and runner. Nose automatically collects tests from Python source files, directories, and packages found in the current working directory. We will focus on how to run individual tests using Nose rather than the whole bunch of tests every time.

Getting ready

First, we need to install the Nose library:

```
$ pip install nose
```

How to do it...

We can execute all the tests in our application using Nose by running the following command:

```
$ nosetests -v
Test creation of new category ... ok
Test creation of new product ... ok
Test home page ... ok
Test Products list page ... ok
Test searching product ... ok
-------------------------------------------------------------------
Ran 5 tests in 0.399s

OK
```

This will pick out all the tests in our application and run them even if we have multiple test files.

To run a single test file, we can simply run the following command:

```
$ nosetests app_tests.py
```

Now, if we want to run a single test, we simply need to run the following command:

```
$ nosetests app_tests:CatalogTestCase.test_home
```

This becomes important when we have a memory-intensive application and a large number of test cases. Then, the tests themselves can take a lot of time to run, and doing so every time can be very frustrating for a developer. Instead, we will prefer to run only those tests that concern the change made or the test that broke on a certain change.

See also

- ► There are many other ways of configuring Nose for optimal and effective usage as per our requirements. Refer to the Nose documentation at `http://nose.readthedocs.org/en/latest/usage.html` for more details.

Using mocking to avoid real API access

We are aware of how testing works, but now, let's say we have a third-party application/service integrated via API calls with our application. It will not be a great idea to make calls to this application/service every time tests are run. Sometimes, these can be paid too, and making calls during tests can not only be expensive, but also affect the statistics of that service. **Mocking** plays a very important role in such scenarios. The simplest example of this can be mocking SMTP for e-mails. In this recipe, we will integrate our application with the `geoip` library and then test it via mocking.

Getting ready

First, we need to install the `mock` and `geoip` libraries and the corresponding database:

```
$ pip install mock
$ pip install python-geoip
$ pip install python-geoip-geolite2
```

Now, let's say we want to store the location of the user who creates a product (think of a scenario where the application is administered via multiple locations around the globe).

We need to make some small changes to `models.py`, `views.py` and `templates/product.html`.

For `models.py`, we will add a new field named `user_timezone`:

```
class Product(db.Model):
    # .. Other fields ..
    user_timezone = db.Column(db.String(255))

    def __init__(self, name, price, category=None, image_path='',
            user_timezone=''):
        .. Other fields initialization ..
        self.user_timezone = user_timezone
```

For `views.py`, we will modify the `create_product()` method to include the timezone:

```
import geoip

def create_product():
    form = ProductForm(request.form)

    if request.method == 'POST' and form.validate():
        # .. Non changed code ..
        match = geoip.geolite2.lookup(request.remote_addr)
```

```
product = Product(
    name, price, company, existing_category, filename,
    match and match.timezone or 'Localhost'
)
# .. Non changed code ..
```

Here, we fetched the geolocation data using an IP lookup and passed this during product creation. If no match is found, then the call is made from the localhost, or from 127.0.0.1 or 0.0.0.0.

Also, we will add this new field in our product template so that it becomes easy to verify in the test. For this, just add {{ product.user_timezone }} somewhere in the product.html template.

How to do it...

Modify app_tests.py to accommodate mocking of the geoip lookup:

```
from geoip import IPInfo
from mock import patch

class CatalogTestCase(unittest.TestCase):

    def setUp(self):
        # .. Non changed code ..
        self.lookup_patcher = patch('geoip.geolite2.lookup',
            autospec=True)
        PatchedLookup = self.lookup_patcher.start()
        PatchedLookup.return_value = IPInfo('17.0.0.1', {
            'location': {
                'time_zone': 'America/Los_Angeles'
            }
        })
        db.create_all()
```

First, we imported IPInfo from geoip, which is the class that defines the format in which the lookup data is to be created. Then, we patched geoip.geolite2.lookup and started the patcher. This means that whenever this call is made, it will be patched with return_value, which is set next. Consider the following code:

```
def tearDown(self):
    self.lookup_patcher.stop()
    os.remove(self.test_db_file)
```

We stopped the mock patcher in `tearDown` so that the actual calls are not affected. Consider the following code:

```python
def test_create_product(self):
    "Test creation of new product"
    # .. Non changed code ..

    rv = self.app.post('/en/product-create', data={
        'name': 'iPhone 5',
        'price': 549.49,
        'company': 'Apple',
        'category': 1
    })
    self.assertEqual(rv.status_code, 302)

    rv = self.app.get('/en/product/1')
    self.assertEqual(rv.status_code, 200)
    self.assertTrue('iPhone 5' in rv.data)
    self.assertTrue('America/Los_Angeles' in rv.data)
```

Here, after the creation of the product, we asserted that the `America/Los_Angeles` value is present somewhere in the product template that is rendered.

How it works...

Run the test and see whether it passes:

```
$ nosetests app_tests:CatalogTestCase.test_create_product -v
Test creation of new product ... ok


----------------------------------------------------

Ran 1 test in 0.095s


OK
```

See also

- ► There are multiple ways in which mocking can be done. I demonstrated just one of them. You can choose any method from the ones available.

Determining test coverage

In the previous recipes, test writing was covered, but there is an important aspect to testing called coverage. Coverage determines how much of our code has been covered by the tests. The higher the percentage of coverage, the better our tests (although it's not the only criterion for good tests). In this recipe, we will check the code coverage of our application.

 Remember that 100 percent test coverage does not mean that the code is flawless. However, in any case, it is better than having no tests or lower coverage. Anything that is not tested is broken.

Getting ready

We will use a library called `coverage` for this recipe. The following is the installation command:

```
$ pip install coverage
```

How to do it...

The simplest way of getting the coverage details is to use the command line. Simply run the following command:

```
$ coverage run –source=../<Folder name of application> --omit=app_tests.py,run.py app_tests.py
```

Here, `--source` indicates the directories that are to be considered in coverage, and `--omit` indicates the files that need to be omitted in the process.

Now, to print the report on the terminal itself, run the following command:

```
$ coverage report
```

The following screenshot shows the output:

Name	Stmts	Miss	Cover
my_app/__init__	31	0	100%
my_app/catalog/__init__	0	0	100%
my_app/catalog/models	69	6	91%
my_app/catalog/views	104	12	88%
TOTAL	204	18	91%

To get a nice HTML output of the coverage report, run the following command:

```
$ coverage html
```

This will create a new folder named `htmlcov` in your current working directory. Inside this, just open up `index.html` in a browser, and the full detailed view will be available.

Alternatively, we can include a piece of code in our test file and get the coverage report every time the tests are run. Add the following code snippets in `app_tests.py`:

Before anything else, add this:

```
import coverage

cov = coverage.coverage(
    omit = [
        '/Users/shalabhaggarwal/workspace/mydev/lib/python2.7/site-
packages/*',
        'app_tests.py'
    ]
)
cov.start()
```

Here, we imported the `coverage` library and created an object of it; this tells the library to omit all `site-packages` (by default, the coverage report is calculated for all dependencies as well) and the test file itself. Then, we started the process to determine the coverage.

Finally, modify the last block of code to the following:

```
if __name__ == '__main__':
    try:
        unittest.main()
    finally:
        cov.stop()
        cov.save()
        cov.report()
        cov.html_report(directory = 'coverage')
        cov.erase()
```

In the preceding code, we first put `unittest.main()` inside a `try..finally` block. This is because `unittest.main()` exits after all the tests are executed. Now, the coverage-specific code is forced to run after this method completes. We first stopped the coverage report, saved it, printed the report on the console, and then generated the HTML version of it before deleting the temporary `.coverage` file (this is created automatically as part of the process).

How it works...

If we run our tests after including the coverage-specific code, then we can run the following command:

```
$ python app_tests.py
```

The output will be as shown in the following screenshot:

Name	Stmts	Miss	Cover	Missing
my_app/__init__	31	0	100%	
my_app/catalog/__init__	0	0	100%	
my_app/catalog/models	69	6	91%	33, 44, 58, 62, 74, 90
my_app/catalog/views	104	12	88%	31, 53-54, 76, 78, 80, 89, 107-108, 147, 161-162
TOTAL	204	18	91%	

See also

▶   It is also possible to determine coverage using the Nose library that we discussed in the *Nose library integration* recipe. I leave it to you to explore this option yourself. Refer to `https://nose.readthedocs.org/en/latest/plugins/cover.html?highlight=coverage` for a head start.

Using profiling to find bottlenecks

Profiling is an important tool when we decide to scale the application. Before scaling, we want to know whether any process is a bottleneck and affects the overall performance. Python has an inbuilt profiler, `cProfile`, that can do the job for us, but to make life easier, Werkzeug has a `ProfilerMiddleware` of its own, which is written over cProfile. We will use this to determine whether there is anything that affects the performance.

Getting ready

We will use the application from the previous recipe and add `ProfilerMiddleware` in a new file named `generate_profile.py`.

How to do it...

Create a new file, `generate_profile.py`, alongside `run.py`, which works like `run.py` itself but with `ProfilerMiddleware`:

```
from werkzeug.contrib.profiler import ProfilerMiddleware
from my_app import app

app.wsgi_app = ProfilerMiddleware(app.wsgi_app, restrictions = [10])
app.run(debug=True)
```

Here, we imported `ProfilerMiddleware` from `werkzeug` and then modified `wsgi_app` on our Flask app to use it, with a restriction of the top 10 calls to be printed in the output.

How it works...

Now, we can run our application using `generate_profile.py`:

```
$ python generate_profile.py
```

We can then create a new product. Then, the output for that specific call will be like the following screenshot:

It is evident from the preceding screenshot that the most intensive call in this process is the call made to the geoip database. So, if we decide to improve the performance sometime down the line, then this is something that needs to be looked at first.

11
Deployment and Post Deployment

Up until now in the book, we have seen how to write Flask applications in different ways. Deployment of an application and managing the application post-deployment is as important as developing it. There can be various ways of deploying an application, where choosing the best way depends on the requirements. Deploying an application correctly is very important from the points of view of security and performance. There are multiple ways of monitoring an application after deployment of which some are paid and others are free to use. Using them again depends on requirements and features offered by them.

In this chapter, we will cover the following recipes:

- ▶ Deploying with Apache
- ▶ Deploying with uWSGI and Nginx
- ▶ Deploying with Gunicorn and Supervisor
- ▶ Deploying with Tornado
- ▶ Using Fabric for deployment
- ▶ S3 storage for file uploads
- ▶ Deploying with Heroku
- ▶ Deploying with AWS Elastic Beanstalk
- ▶ Application monitoring with Pingdom
- ▶ Application performance management and monitoring with New Relic

Introduction

In this chapter, we will talk about various application-deployment techniques, followed by some monitoring tools that are used post-deployment.

Each of the tools and techniques has its own set of features. For example, adding too much monitoring to an application can prove to be an extra overhead to the application and the developers as well. Similarly, missing out on monitoring can lead to undetected user errors and overall user dissatisfaction.

Hence, we should choose the tools wisely and they will ease our lives to the maximum.

In the post-deployment monitoring tools, we will discuss Pingdom and New Relic. Sentry is another tool that will prove to be the most beneficial of all from a developer's perspective. It has already been covered in the *Using Sentry to monitor exceptions* recipe in *Chapter 10, Debugging, Error Handling, and Testing*.

Deploying with Apache

First, we will learn how to deploy a Flask application with Apache, which is, unarguably, the most popular HTTP server. For Python web applications, we will use mod_wsgi, which implements a simple Apache module that can host any Python applications that support the WSGI interface.

 Remember that mod_wsgi is not the same as Apache and needs to be installed separately.

Getting ready

We will start with our catalog application and make appropriate changes to it to make it deployable using the Apache HTTP server.

First, we should make our application installable so that our application and all its libraries are on the Python load path. This can be done using a `setup.py` script, as seen in the *Making a Flask app installable using setuptools* recipe in *Chapter 1, Flask Configurations*. There will be a few changes to the script as per this application. The major changes are mentioned here:

```
packages=[
    'my_app',
    'my_app.catalog',
],
include_package_data=True,
zip_safe = False,
```

First, we mentioned all the packages that need to be installed as part of our application. Each of these needs to have an __init__.py file. The zip_safe flag tells the installer to not install this application as a ZIP file. The include_package_data statement reads from a MANIFEST.in file in the same folder and includes any package data mentioned here. Our MANIFEST.in file looks like:

```
recursive-include my_app/templates *
recursive-include my_app/static *
recursive-include my_app/translations *
```

Now, just install the application using the following command:

```
$ python setup.py install
```

> Installing mod_wsgi is usually OS-specific. Installing it on a Debian-based distribution should be as easy as just using the packaging tool, that is, apt or aptitude. For details, refer to https://code.google.com/p/modwsgi/wiki/InstallationInstructions and https://github.com/GrahamDumpleton/mod_wsgi.

How to do it...

We need to create some more files, the first one being app.wsgi. This loads our application as a WSGI application:

```
activate_this = '<Path to virtualenv>/bin/activate_this.py'
execfile(activate_this, dict(__file__=activate_this))

from my_app import app as application
import sys, logging
logging.basicConfig(stream = sys.stderr)
```

As we perform all our installations inside virtualenv, we need to activate the environment before our application is loaded. In the case of system-wide installations, the first two statements are not needed. Then, we need to import our app object as application, which is used as the application being served. The last two lines are optional, as they just stream the output to the standard logger, which is disabled by mod_wsgi by default.

> The app object needs to be imported as application, because mod_wsgi expects the application keyword.

Next comes a config file that will be used by the Apache HTTP server to serve our application correctly from specific locations. The file is named `apache_wsgi.conf`:

```
<VirtualHost *>

    WSGIScriptAlias / <Path to application>/flask_catalog_deployment/
app.wsgi

    <Directory <Path to application>/flask_catalog_deployment>
        Order allow,deny
        Allow from all
    </Directory>

</VirtualHost>
```

The preceding code is the Apache configuration, which tells the HTTP server about the various directories where the application has to be loaded from.

The final step is to add the `apache_wsgi.conf` file to `apache2/httpd.conf` so that our application is loaded when the server runs:

```
Include <Path to application>/flask_catalog_deployment/
  apache_wsgi.conf
```

How it works...

Let's restart the Apache server service using the following command:

```
$ sudo apachectl restart
```

Open up `http://127.0.0.1/` in the browser to see the application's home page. Any errors coming up can be seen at `/var/log/apache2/error_log` (this path can differ depending on OS).

There's more...

After all this, it is possible that the product images uploaded as part of the product creation do not work. For this, we should make a small modification to our application's configuration:

```
app.config['UPLOAD_FOLDER'] = '<Some static absolute
  path>/flask_test_uploads'
```

We opted for a static path because we do not want it to change every time the application is modified or installed.

Now, we will include the path chosen in the preceding code to `apache_wsgi.conf`:

```
Alias /static/uploads/ "<Some static absolute
  path>/flask_test_uploads/"
<Directory "<Some static absolute path>/flask_test_uploads">
    Order allow,deny
    Options Indexes
    Allow from all
    IndexOptions FancyIndexing
</Directory>
```

After this, install the application and restart `apachectl`.

See also

▸ http://httpd.apache.org/

▸ https://code.google.com/p/modwsgi/

▸ http://wsgi.readthedocs.org/en/latest/

▸ https://pythonhosted.org/setuptools/setuptools.html#setting-the-zip-safe-flag

Deploying with uWSGI and Nginx

For those who are already aware of the usefulness of uWSGI and Nginx, there is not much that can be explained. uWSGI is a protocol as well as an application server and provides a complete stack to build hosting services. Nginx is a reverse proxy and HTTP server that is very lightweight and capable of handling virtually unlimited requests. Nginx works seamlessly with uWSGI and provides many under-the-hood optimizations for better performance.

Getting ready

We will use our application from the last recipe, *Deploying with Apache*, and use the same `app.wsgi`, `setup.py`, and `MANIFEST.in` files. Also, other changes made to the application's configuration in the last recipe will apply to this recipe as well.

 Disable any other HTTP servers that might be running, such as Apache and so on.

How to do it...

First, we need to install uWSGI and Nginx. On Debian-based distributions such as Ubuntu, they can be easily installed using the following commands:

```
# sudo apt-get install nginx
# sudo apt-get install uWSGI
```

 You can also install uWSGI inside a `virtualenv` using the `pip install uWSGI` command.

Again, these are OS-specific, so refer to the respective documentations as per the OS used.

Make sure that you have an `apps-enabled` folder for uWSGI, where we will keep our application-specific uWSGI configuration files, and a `sites-enabled` folder for Nginx, where we will keep our site-specific configuration files. Usually, these are already present in most installations in the `/etc/` folder. If not, refer to the OS-specific documentations to figure out the same.

Next, we will create a file named `uwsgi.ini` in our application:

```
[uwsgi]
http-socket    = :9090
plugin     = python
wsgi-file = <Path to application>/flask_catalog_deployment/app.wsgi
processes    = 3
```

To test whether uWSGI is working as expected, run the following command:

```
$ uwsgi --ini uwsgi.ini
```

The preceding file and command are equivalent to running the following command:

```
$ uwsgi --http-socket :9090 --plugin python --wsgi-file app.wsgi
```

Now, point your browser to `http://127.0.0.1:9090/`; this should open up the home page of the application.

Create a soft link of this file to the `apps-enabled` folder mentioned earlier using the following command:

```
$ ln -s <path/to/uwsgi.ini> <path/to/apps-enabled>
```

Before moving ahead, edit the preceding file to replace `http-socket` with `socket`. This changes the protocol from HTTP to uWSGI (read more about it at `http://uwsgi-docs.readthedocs.org/en/latest/Protocol.html`). Now, create a new file called `nginx-wsgi.conf`. This contains the Nginx configuration needed to serve our application and the static content:

```
location / {
    include uwsgi_params;
    uwsgi_pass 127.0.0.1:9090;
}
location /static/uploads/{
    alias <Some static absolute path>/flask_test_uploads/;
}
```

In the preceding code block, `uwsgi_pass` specifies the uWSGI server that needs to be mapped to the specified location.

Create a soft link of this file to the `sites-enabled` folder mentioned earlier using the following command:

$ ln -s <path/to/nginx-wsgi.conf> <path/to/sites-enabled>

Edit the `nginx.conf` file (usually found at `/etc/nginx/nginx.conf`) to add the following line inside the first server block before the last `}`:

```
include <path/to/sites-enabled>/*;
```

After all of this, reload the Nginx server using the following command:

$ sudo nginx -s reload

Point your browser to `http://127.0.0.1/` to see the application that is served via Nginx and uWSGI.

 The preceding instructions of this recipe can vary depending on the OS being used and different versions of the same OS can also impact the paths and commands used. Different versions of these packages can also have some variations in usage. Refer to the documentation links provided in the next section.

See also

▸ Refer to `http://uwsgi-docs.readthedocs.org/en/latest/` for more information on uWSGI.

▸ Refer to `http://nginx.com/` for more information on Nginx.

- ▶ There is a good article by DigitalOcean on this. I advise you to go through this to have a better understanding of the topic. It is available at `https://www.digitalocean.com/community/tutorials/how-to-deploy-python-wsgi-applications-using-uwsgi-web-server-with-nginx`.

- ▶ To get an insight into the difference between Apache and Nginx, I think the article by Anturis at `https://anturis.com/blog/nginx-vs-apache/` is pretty good.

Deploying with Gunicorn and Supervisor

Gunicorn is a WSGI HTTP server for Unix. It is very simple to implement, ultra light, and fairly speedy. Its simplicity lies in its broad compatibility with various web frameworks.

Supervisor is a monitoring tool that controls various child processes and handles the starting/restarting of these child processes when they exit abruptly due to some reason. It can be extended to control the processes via the XML-RPC API over remote locations without logging in to the server (we won't discuss this here as it is out of the scope of this book).

One thing to remember is that these tools can be used along with the other tools mentioned in the applications in the previous recipe, such as using Nginx as a proxy server. This is left to you to try on your own.

Getting ready

We will start with the installation of both the packages, that is, `gunicorn` and `supervisor`. Both can be directly installed using `pip`:

```
$ pip install gunicorn
$ pip install supervisor
```

How to do it...

To check whether the `gunicorn` package works as expected, just run the following command from inside our application folder:

```
$ gunicorn -w 4 -b 127.0.0.1:8000 my_app:app
```

After this, point your browser to `http://127.0.0.1:8000/` to see the application's home page.

Now, we need to do the same using Supervisor so that this runs as a daemon and will be controlled by Supervisor itself rather than human intervention. First of all, we need a Supervisor configuration file. This can be achieved by running the following command from `virtualenv`. Supervisor, by default, looks for an `etc` folder that has a file named `supervisord.conf`. In system-wide installations, this folder is `/etc/`, and in `virtualenv`, it will look for an `etc` folder in `virtualenv` and then fall back to `/etc/`:

```
$ echo_supervisord_conf > etc/supervisord.conf
```

 The `echo_supervisord_conf` program is provided by Supervisor; it prints a sample config file to the location specified.

This command will create a file named `supervisord.conf` in the `etc` folder. Add the following block in this file:

```
[program:flask_catalog]
command=<path/to/virtualenv>/bin/gunicorn -w 4 -b 127.0.0.1:8000 my_
app:app
directory=<path/to/virtualenv>/flask_catalog_deployment
user=someuser # Relevant user
autostart=true
autorestart=true
stdout_logfile=/tmp/app.log
stderr_logfile=/tmp/error.log
```

 Make a note that one should never run the applications as a root user. This is a huge security flaw in itself as the application crashes, which can harm the OS itself.

How it works...

Now, run the following commands:

```
$ supervisord
$ supervisorctl status
flask_catalog    RUNNING    pid 40466, uptime 0:00:03
```

The first command invokes the `supervisord` server, and the next one gives a status of all the child processes.

 The tools discussed in this recipe can be coupled with Nginx to serve as a reverse proxy server. I suggest that you try it by yourself.

Every time you make a change to your application and then wish to restart Gunicorn in order for it to reflect the changes, run the following command:

```
$ supervisorctl restart all
```

You can also give specific processes instead of restarting everything:

```
$ supervisorctl restart flask_catalog
```

See also

▶ http://gunicorn-docs.readthedocs.org/en/latest/index.html
▶ http://supervisord.org/index.html

Deploying with Tornado

Tornado is a complete web framework and a standalone web server in itself. Here, we will use Flask to create our application, which is basically a combination of URL routing and templating, and leave the server part to Tornado. Tornado is built to hold thousands of simultaneous standing connections and makes applications very scalable.

 Tornado has limitations while working with WSGI applications. So, choose wisely! Read more at http://www.tornadoweb.org/en/stable/wsgi.html#running-wsgi-apps-on-tornado-servers.

Getting ready

Installing Tornado can be simply done using `pip`:

```
$ pip install tornado
```

How to do it...

Next, create a file named `tornado_server.py` and put the following code in it:

```python
from tornado.wsgi import WSGIContainer
from tornado.httpserver import HTTPServer
from tornado.ioloop import IOLoop
from my_app import app

http_server = HTTPServer(WSGIContainer(app))
http_server.listen(5000)
IOLoop.instance().start()
```

Here, we created a WSGI container for our application; this container is then used to create an HTTP server, and the application is hosted on port 5000.

How it works...

Run the Python file created in the previous section using the following command:

```
$ python tornado_server.py
```

Point your browser to `http://127.0.0.1:5000/` to see the home page being served.

 We can couple Tornado with Nginx (as a reverse proxy to serve static content) and Supervisor (as a process manager) for the best results. It is left for you to try this on your own.

Using Fabric for deployment

Fabric is a command-line tool in Python; it streamlines the use of SSH for application deployment or system-administration tasks. As it allows the execution of shell commands on remote servers, the overall process of deployment is simplified, as the whole process can now be condensed into a Python file, which can be run whenever needed. Therefore, it saves the pain of logging in to the server and manually running commands every time an update has to be made.

Getting ready

Installing Fabric can be simply done using `pip`:

```
$ pip install fabric
```

We will use the application from the *Deploying with Gunicorn and Supervisor* recipe. We will create a Fabric file to perform the same process to the remote server.

For simplicity, let's assume that the remote server setup has been already done and all the required packages have also been installed with a `virtualenv` environment, which has also been created.

How to do it...

First, we need to create a file called `fabfile.py` in our application, preferably at the application's root directory, that is, along with the `setup.py` and `run.py` files. Fabric, by default, expects this filename. If we use a different filename, then it will have to be explicitly specified while executing.

A basic Fabric file will look like:

```python
from fabric.api import sudo, cd, prefix, run

def deploy_app():
    "Deploy to the server specified"
    root_path = '/usr/local/my_env'

    with cd(root_path):
        with prefix("source %s/bin/activate" % root_path):
            with cd('flask_catalog_deployment'):
                run('git pull')
                run('python setup.py install')

                sudo('bin/supervisorctl restart all')
```

Here, we first moved into our `virtualenv`, activated it, and then moved into our application. Then, the code is pulled from the Git repository, and the updated application code is installed using `setup.py install`. After this, we restarted the supervisor processes so that the updated application is now rendered by the server.

> Most of the commands used here are self-explanatory, except `prefix`, which wraps all the succeeding commands in its block with the command provided. This means that the command to activate `virtualenv` will run first and then all the commands in the `with` block will execute with `virtualenv` activated. The `virtualenv` will be deactivated as soon as control goes out of the `with` block.

How it works...

To run this file, we need to provide the remote server where the script will be executed. So, the command will look something like:

```
$ fab -H my.remote.server deploy_app
```

Here, we specified the address of the remote host where we wish to deploy and the name of the method to be called from the `fab` script.

There's more...

We can also specify the remote host inside our `fab` script, and this can be good idea if the deployment server remains the same most of the times. To do this, add the following code to the `fab` script:

```
from fabric.api import settings

def deploy_app_to_server():
    "Deploy to the server hardcoded"
    with settings(host_string='my.remote.server'):
        deploy_app()
```

Here, we have hardcoded the host and then called the method we created earlier to start the deployment process.

S3 storage for file uploads

Amazon explains S3 as the storage for the Internet that is designed to make web-scale computing easier for developers. S3 provides a very simple interface via web services; this makes storage and retrieval of any amount of data very simple at any time from anywhere on the Internet. Until now, in our catalog application, we saw that there were issues in managing the product images uploaded as a part of the creating process. The whole headache will go away if the images are stored somewhere globally and are easily accessible from anywhere. We will use S3 for the same purpose.

Getting ready

Amazon offers **boto**, a complete Python library that interfaces with Amazon Web Services via web services. Almost all of the AWS features can be controlled using boto. It can be installed using `pip`:

```
$ pip install boto
```

How to do it...

Now, we should make some changes to our existing catalog application to accommodate support for file uploads and retrieval from S3.

First, we need to store the AWS-specific configuration to allow boto to make calls to S3. Add the following statements to the application's configuration file, that is, `my_app/__init__.py`:

```
app.config['AWS_ACCESS_KEY'] = 'Amazon Access Key'
app.config['AWS_SECRET_KEY'] = 'Amazon Secret Key'
app.config['AWS_BUCKET'] = 'flask-cookbook'
```

Next, we need to change our `views.py` file:

```
from boto.s3.connection import S3Connection
```

This is the import that we need from boto. Next, replace the following two lines in `create_product()`:

```
filename = secure_filename(image.filename)
image.save(os.path.join(app.config['UPLOAD_FOLDER'], filename))
```

Replace these two lines with:

```
filename = image.filename
conn = S3Connection(
    app.config['AWS_ACCESS_KEY'], app.config['AWS_SECRET_KEY']
)
bucket = conn.create_bucket(app.config['AWS_BUCKET'])
key = bucket.new_key(filename)
key.set_contents_from_file(image)
key.make_public()
key.set_metadata(
    'Content-Type', 'image/' + filename.split('.')[-1].lower()
)
```

The last change will go to our `product.html` template, where we need to change the image src path. Replace the original `img src` statement with the following statement:

```
<img src="{{ 'https://s3.amazonaws.com/' + config['AWS_BUCKET'] +
    '/' + product.image_path }}"/>
```

How it works...

Now, run the application as usual and create a product. When the created product is rendered, the product image will take a bit of time to come up as it is now being served from S3 (and not from a local machine). If this happens, then the integration with S3 has been successfully done.

See also

► The next recipe, *Deploying with Heroku*, to see how S3 is instrumental in easy deployment without the hassles of managing uploads on the server

Deploying with Heroku

Heroku is a cloud application platform that provides an easy and quick way to build and deploy web applications. Heroku manages the servers, deployment, and related operations while developers spend their time on developing applications. Deploying with Heroku is pretty simple with the help of the Heroku toolbelt, which is a bundle of some tools that make deployment with Heroku a cakewalk.

Getting ready

We will proceed with the application from the previous recipe that has S3 support for uploads.

As mentioned earlier, the first step will be to download the Heroku toolbelt, which can be downloaded as per the OS from `https://toolbelt.heroku.com/`.

Once the toolbelt is installed, a certain set of commands will be available at the terminal; we will see them later in this recipe.

 It is advised that you perform Heroku deployment from a fresh `virtualenv` where we have only the required packages for our application installed and nothing else. This will make the deployment process faster and easier.

Now, run the following command to log in to your Heroku account and sync your machined SSH key with the server:

```
$ heroku login
Enter your Heroku credentials.
Email: shalabh7777@gmail.com
Password (typing will be hidden):
Authentication successful.
```

You will be prompted to create a new SSH key if one does not exist. Proceed accordingly.

 Remember! Before all this, you need to have a Heroku account available on `https://www.heroku.com/`.

How to do it...

Now, we already have an application that needs to be deployed to Heroku. First, Heroku needs to know the command that it needs to run while deploying the application. This is done in a file named `Procfile`:

```
web: gunicorn -w 4 my_app:app
```

Here, we will tell Heroku to run this command to run our web application.

 There are a lot of different configurations and commands that can go into `Procfile`. For more details, read the Heroku documentation.

Heroku needs to know the dependencies that need to be installed in order to successfully install and run our application. This is done via the `requirements.txt` file:

```
Flask==0.10.1
Flask-Restless==0.14.0
Flask-SQLAlchemy==1.0
Flask-WTF==0.10.0
Jinja2==2.7.3
MarkupSafe==0.23
SQLAlchemy==0.9.7
WTForms==2.0.1
Werkzeug==0.9.6
boto==2.32.1
```

```
gunicorn==19.1.1
itsdangerous==0.24
mimerender==0.5.4
python-dateutil==2.2
python-geoip==1.2
python-geoip-geolite2==2014.0207
python-mimeparse==0.1.4
six==1.7.3
wsgiref==0.1.2
```

This file contains all the dependencies of our application, the dependencies of these dependencies, and so on. An easy way to generate this file is using the `pip freeze` command:

```
$ pip freeze > requirements.txt
```

This will create/update the `requirements.txt` file with all the packages installed in `virtualenv`.

Now, we need to create a Git repo of our application. For this, we will run the following commands:

```
$ git init
```

```
$ git add .
```

```
$ git commit -m "First Commit"
```

Now, we have a Git repo with all our files added.

 Make sure that you have a `.gitignore` file in your repo or at a global level to prevent temporary files such as `.pyc` from being added to the repo.

Now, we need to create a Heroku application and push our application to Heroku:

```
$ heroku create
```

```
Creating damp-tor-6795... done, stack is cedar
```

```
http://damp-tor-6795.herokuapp.com/ | git@heroku.com:damp-tor-
  6795.git
```

```
Git remote heroku added
```

```
$ git push heroku master
```

After the last command, a whole lot of stuff will get printed on the terminal; this will indicate all the packages being installed and finally, the application being launched.

How it works...

After the previous commands have successfully finished, just open up the URL provided by Heroku at the end of deployment in a browser or run the following command:

```
$ heroku open
```

This will open up the application's home page. Try creating a new product with an image and see the image being served from Amazon S3.

To see the logs of the application, run the following command:

```
$ heroku logs
```

There's more...

There is a glitch with the deployment we just did. Every time we update the deployment via the `git push` command, the SQLite database gets overwritten. The solution to this is to use the Postgres setup provided by Heroku itself. I urge you to try this by yourself.

Deploying with AWS Elastic Beanstalk

In the last recipe, we saw how deployment to servers becomes easy with Heroku. Similarly, Amazon has a service named Elastic Beanstalk, which allows developers to deploy their application to Amazon EC2 instances as easily as possible. With just a few configuration options, a Flask application can be deployed to AWS using Elastic Beanstalk in a couple of minutes.

Getting ready

We will start with our catalog application from the previous recipe, *Deploying with Heroku*. The only file that remains the same from this recipe is `requirement.txt`. The rest of the files that were added as a part of that recipe can be ignored or discarded for this recipe.

Now, the first thing that we need to do is download the AWS Elastic Beanstalk command-line tool library from the Amazon website (`http://aws.amazon.com/code/6752709412171743`). This will download a ZIP file that needs to be unzipped and placed in a suitable place, preferably your workspace home.

The path of this tool should be added to the `PATH` environment so that the commands are available throughout. This can be done via the `export` command as shown:

```
$ export PATH=$PATH:<path to unzipped EB CLI package>/eb/linux/python2.7/
```

This can also be added to the ~/.profile or ~/.bash_profile file using:

```
export PATH=$PATH:<path to unzipped EB CLI package>/eb/linux/
python2.7/
```

How to do it...

There are a few conventions that need to be followed in order to deploy using Beanstalk. Beanstalk assumes that there will be a file called application.py, which contains the application object (in our case, the app object). Beanstalk treats this file as the WSGI file, and this is used for deployment.

> In the *Deploying with Apache* recipe, we had a file named app.wgsi where we referred our app object as application because apache/mod_wsgi needed it to be so. The same thing happens here too because Amazon, by default, deploys using Apache behind the scenes.

The contents of this application.py file can be just a few lines as shown here:

```
from my_app import app as application
import sys, logging
logging.basicConfig(stream = sys.stderr)
```

Now, create a Git repo in the application and commit with all the files added:

```
$ git init
$ git add .
$ git commit -m "First Commit"
```

> Make sure that you have a .gitignore file in your repo or at a global level to prevent temporary files such as .pyc from being added to the repo.

Now, we need to deploy to Elastic Beanstalk. Run the following command to do this:

```
$ eb init
```

The preceding command initializes the process for the configuration of your Elastic Beanstalk instance. It will ask for the AWS credentials followed by a lot of other configuration options needed for the creation of the EC2 instance, which can be selected as needed. For more help on these options, refer to http://docs.aws.amazon.com/elasticbeanstalk/latest/dg/create_deploy_Python_flask.html.

After this is done, run the following command to trigger the creation of servers, followed by the deployment of the application:

```
$ eb start
```

 Behind the scenes, the preceding command creates the EC2 instance (a volume), assigns an elastic IP, and then runs the following command to push our application to the newly created server for deployment:
```
$ git aws.push
```

This will take a few minutes to complete. When done, you can check the status of your application using the following command:

```
$ eb status -verbose
```

Whenever you need to update your application, just commit your changes using the `git` and `push` commands as follows:

```
$ git aws.push
```

How it works...

When the deployment process finishes, it gives out the application URL. Point your browser to it to see the application being served.

Yet, you will find a small glitch with the application. The static content, that is, the CSS and JS code, is not being served. This is because the static path is not correctly comprehended by Beanstalk. This can be simply fixed by modifying the application's configuration on your application's monitoring/configuration page in the AWS management console. See the following screenshots to understand this better:

Click on the **Configuration** menu item in the left-hand side menu.

Notice the highlighted box in the preceding screenshot. This is what we need to change as per our application. Open **Software Settings**.

Change the virtual path for /static/, as shown in the preceding screenshot.

After this change is made, the environment created by Elastic Beanstalk will be updated automatically, although it will take a bit of time. When done, check the application again to see the static content also being served correctly.

Application monitoring with Pingdom

Pingdom is a website-monitoring tool that has the USP of notifying you as soon as your website goes down. The basic idea behind this tool is to constantly ping the website at a specific interval, say, 30 seconds. If a ping fails, it will notify you via an e-mail, SMS, tweet, or push notifications to mobile apps, which inform that your site is down. It will keep on pinging at a faster rate until the site is back up again. There are other monitoring features too, but we will limit ourselves to uptime checks in this book.

Getting ready

As Pingdom is a SaaS service, the first step will be to sign up for an account. Pingdom offers a free trial of 1 month in case you just want to try it out. The website for the service is `https://www.pingdom.com`.

We will use the application deployed to AWS in the *Deploying with AWS Elastic Beanstalk* recipe to check for uptime. Here, Pingdom will send an e-mail in case the application goes down and will send an e-mail again when it is back up.

How to do it...

After successful registration, create a check for time. Have a look at the following screenshot:

As you can see, I already added a check for the AWS instance. To create a new check, click on the **ADD NEW** button. Fill in the details asked by the form that comes up.

How it works...

After the check is successfully created, try to break the application by consciously making a mistake somewhere in the code and then deploying to AWS. As soon as the faulty application is deployed, you will get an e-mail notifying you of this. This e-mail will look like:

Once the application is fixed and put back up again, the next e-mail should look like:

UP alert: Flask AWS (flaskcatalogeb-env-gqcu2i5bbm.elasticbeanstalk.com) is UP

Inbox   x

alert@pingdom.com   4:46 PM (11 minutes ago)

to me

PingdomAlert UP:
 Flask AWS (flaskcatalogeb-env-gqcu2i5bbm.elasticbeanstalk.com) is UP again at 08/20/2014 12:16:23PM, after 4m of
 downtime.

You can also check how long the application has been up and the downtime instances from the Pingdom administration panel.

Application performance management and monitoring with New Relic

New Relic is an analytics software that provides near real-time operational and business analytics related to your application. It provides deep analytics on the behavior of the application from various aspects. It does the job of a profiler as well as eliminating the need to maintain extra moving parts in the application. It actually works in a scenario where our application sends data to New Relic rather than New Relic asking for statistics from our application.

Getting ready

We will use the application from the last recipe, which is deployed to AWS.

The first step will be to sign up with New Relic for an account. Follow the simple signup process, and upon completion and e-mail verification, it will lead to your dashboard. Here, you will have your license key available, which we will use later to connect our application to this account. The dashboard should look like the following screenshot:

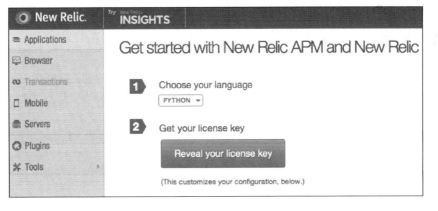

Here, click on the large button named **Reveal your license key**.

How to do it...

Once we have the license key, we need to install the `newrelic` Python library:

```
$ pip install newrelic
```

Now, we need to generate a file called `newrelic.ini`, which will contain details regarding the license key, the name of our application, and so on. This can be done using the following commands:

```
$ newrelic-admin generate-config LICENSE-KEY newrelic.ini
```

In the preceding command, replace `LICENSE-KEY` with the actual license key of your account. Now, we have a new file called `newrelic.ini`. Open and edit the file for the application name and anything else as needed.

To check whether the `newrelic.ini` file is working successfully, run the following command:

```
$ newrelic-admin validate-config newrelic.ini
```

This will tell us whether the validation was successful or not. If not, then check the license key and its validity.

Now, add the following lines at the top of the application's configuration file, that is, `my_app/__init__.py` in our case. Make sure that you add these lines before anything else is imported:

```
    import newrelic.agent
    newrelic.agent.initialize('newrelic.ini')
```

Now, we need to update the `requirements.txt` file. So, run the following command:

```
$ pip freeze > requirements.txt
```

After this, commit the changes and deploy the application to AWS using the following command:

```
$ git aws.push
```

How it works...

Once the application is successfully updated on AWS, it will start sending statistics to New Relic, and the dashboard will have a new application added to it.

Open the application-specific page, and a whole lot of statistics will come across. It will also show which calls have taken the most amount of time and how the application is performing. You will also see multiple tabs that correspond to a different type of monitoring to cover all the aspects.

See also

▶ The *Deploying with AWS Elastic Beanstalk* recipe to understand the deployment part used in this recipe

12

Other Tips and Tricks

This book has covered almost all the areas needed to be known for the creation of a web application using Flask. Much has been covered, and you need to explore more on your own. In this final chapter, we will go through some additional recipes that can be used to add value to the application, if necessary.

In this chapter, we will cover the following recipes:

- ▶ Full-text search with Whoosh
- ▶ Full-text search with Elasticsearch
- ▶ Working with signals
- ▶ Using caching with your application
- ▶ E-mail support for Flask applications
- ▶ Understanding asynchronous operations
- ▶ Working with Celery

Introduction

In this chapter, we will first learn how to implement full-text search using Whoosh and Elasticsearch. Full-text search becomes important for a web application that offers a lot of content and options, such as an e-commerce site. Next, we will catch up on signals that help decouple applications by sending notifications (signals) when an action is performed somewhere in the application. This action is caught by a subscriber/receiver, which can perform an action accordingly. This is followed by implementing caching for our Flask application.

We will also see how e-mail support is added to our application and how e-mails can be sent directly from the application on different actions. We will then see how we can make our application asynchronous. By default, WSGI applications are synchronous and blocking, that is, by default, they do not serve multiple simultaneous requests together. We will see how to deal with this via a small example. We will also integrate Celery with our application and see how a task queue can be used to our application's benefit.

Full-text search with Whoosh

Whoosh is a fast, *featureful*, full-text indexing and searching library implemented in Python. It has a pure Pythonic API and allows developers to add search functionality to their applications easily and efficiently. In this recipe, we will use a package called Flask-WhooshAlchemy, which integrates the text-search functionality of Whoosh with SQLAlchemy for use in Flask applications.

Getting ready

The Flask-WhooshAlchemy package can be installed via `pip` using the following command:

```
$ pip install flask_whooshalchemy
```

This will install the required packages and dependencies.

How to do it...

Integrating Whoosh with Flask using SQLAlchemy is pretty straightforward. First, we need to provide the path to the Whoosh base directory where the index for our models will be created. This should be done in the application's configuration, that is, `my_app/__init__.py`:

```
app.config['WHOOSH_BASE'] = '/tmp/whoosh'
```

You can choose any path you prefer, and it can be absolute or relative.

Next, we need to make some changes to our `models.py` file to make the string/text fields searchable:

```
import flask.ext.whooshalchemy as whooshalchemy
from my_app import app


class Product(db.Model):
    __searchable__ = ['name', 'company']
    # ... Rest of code as before ... #


whooshalchemy.whoosh_index(app, Product)


class Category(db.Model):
```

```
        __searchable__ = ['name']
        # … Rest of code as before … #

    whooshalchemy.whoosh_index(app, Category)
```

Notice the __searchable__ statement that has been added to both the models. It tells Whoosh to create index on these fields. Remember that these fields should only be of the text or string type. The whoosh_index statements tell the application to create the index for these models if they are not already available.

After this is done, we can add a new handler to search using Whoosh. This is to be done in views.py:

```
@catalog.route('/product-search-whoosh')
@catalog.route('/product-search-whoosh/<int:page>')
def product_search_whoosh(page=1):
    q = request.args.get('q')
    products = Product.query.whoosh_search(q)
    return render_template(
        'products.html', products=products.paginate(page, 10)
    )
```

Here, we got the URL argument with the key as q and passed its value to the whoosh_search() method that does the full-text search in the Product model on the name and company fields, which we had made searchable in the models earlier.

How it works...

Those who have gone through the *SQL-based searching* recipe in *Chapter 4, Working with Views,* will recall that we implemented a method that performed a search on the basis of fields. However, here, in the case of Whoosh, we do not need to specify any field while searching. We can type any text and if this matches the searchable fields, the results will be shown, ordered in the rank of their relevance.

First, create some products in the application. Now, if we open http://127.0.0.1:5000/product-search-whoosh?q=iPhone, the resulting page will list all the products that have iPhone in their names.

> There are advanced options provided by Whoosh where we can control which fields to be searched for or how the result has to be ordered. You can explore them as per the needs of your application.

See also

▸ Refer to `https://pythonhosted.org/Whoosh/`

▸ Refer to `https://pypi.python.org/pypi/Flask-WhooshAlchemy`

Full-text search with Elasticsearch

Elasticsearch is a search server based on Lucene, which is an open source information-retrieval library. Elasticsearch provides a distributed full-text search engine with a RESTful web interface and schema-free JSON documents. In this recipe, we will implement full-text search using Elasticsearch for our Flask application.

Getting ready

We will use a Python library called `pyelasticsearch`, which makes dealing with Elasticsearch a lot easier:

```
$ pip install pyelasticsearch
```

We also need to install the Elasticsearch server itself. This can be downloaded from `http://www.elasticsearch.org/download/`. Unpack the package downloaded and run the following command:

```
$ bin/elasticsearch
```

This will start the Elasticsearch server on `http://localhost:9200/` by default.

How to do it...

To perform the integration, we will start by adding the Elasticsearch object to the application's configuration, that is, `my_app/__init__.py`:

```python
from pyelasticsearch import ElasticSearch
from pyelasticsearch.exceptions import IndexAlreadyExistsError

es = ElasticSearch('http://localhost:9200/')
try:
    es.create_index('catalog')
except IndexAlreadyExistsError, e:
    pass
```

Here, we created an `es` object from the `ElasticSearch` class, which accepts the server URL. Then, we created an index called `catalog`. This is done in a `try-except` block because if the index already exists, then `IndexAlreadyExistsError` is thrown, which we can just ignore.

Next, we need the ability to add a document to our Elasticsearch index. This can be done in views or models, but in my opinion, the best way will be to add it in the model layer. So, we will do this in the `models.py` file:

```python
from my_app import es

class Product(db.Model):

    def add_index_to_es(self):
        es.index('catalog', 'product', {
            'name': self.name,
            'category': self.category.name
        })
        es.refresh('catalog')

class Category(db.Model):

    def add_index_to_es(self):
        es.index('catalog', 'category', {
            'name': self.name,
        })
        es.refresh('catalog')
```

Here, in each of the models, we added a new method called `add_index_to_es()`, which will add the document that corresponds to the current `Product` or `Category` object to the `catalog` index with the relevant document type, that is, `product` or `category`. Finally, we refreshed our index so that the newly created index is available to be searched for.

The `add_index_to_es()` method can be called when we create, update, or delete a product or category. For demonstration purposes, I will just add this method while creating the product in `views.py`:

```python
from my_app import es

def create_product():
    #... normal product creation as always ...#
    db.session.commit()
    product.add_index_to_es()
    #... normal process as always ...#

@catalog.route('/product-search-es')
@catalog.route('/product-search-es/<int:page>')
def product_search_es(page=1):
    q = request.args.get('q')
    products = es.search(q)
    return products
```

Also, we added a `product_search_es()` method to allow searching on the Elasticsearch index we just created. Do the same in the `create_category()` method as well.

How to do it...

Now, let's say we created a few categories and products in each of the categories. Now, if we open `http://127.0.0.1:5000/product-search-es?q=galaxy`, then we will get a response like what is shown in the following screenshot:

```
{"hits": {"hits": [{"_score": 0.7554128, "_type": "product", "_id":
"ceuE9YqYSVO6LIz43acxVg", "_source": {"category": "Phones",
"company": "Samsung", "name": "Galaxy S5"}, "_index": "catalog"},
{"_score": 0.7554128, "_type": "product", "_id":
"xtLtchRzTCmyKZY91FTEew", "_source": {"category": "Phones", "name":
"Galaxy S5"}, "_index": "catalog"}], "total": 2, "max_score": 0.7554128},
"_shards": {"successful": 10, "failed": 0, "total": 10}, "took": 2, "timed_out":
false}
```

I encourage you to try and enhance the formatting and display of the page.

Working with signals

Signals can be thought of as events that happen in our application. These events can be subscribed by certain receivers who then invoke a function whenever the event occurs. The occurrence of events is broadcasted by senders who can specify the arguments that can be used by the function to be triggered by the receiver.

 You should refrain from modifying any application data in the signals because signals are not executed in a specified order and can easily lead to data corruption.

Getting ready

We will use a Python library called `blinker`, which provides the signals feature. Flask has inbuilt support for `blinker` and uses signaling to a good extent. There are certain core signals provided by Flask.

In this recipe, we will use the application from the *Full-text search with Elasticsearch* recipe and make the addition of the `product` and `category` documents to indexes work via signals.

How to do it...

First, we need to create signals for the product and category creation. This can be done in `models.py`. This can be done in any file we want, as signals are created on the global scope:

```
from blinker import Namespace

catalog_signals = Namespace()
product_created = catalog_signals.signal('product-created')
category_created = catalog_signals.signal('category-created')
```

We use `Namespace` to create signals, as it will create them in a custom namespace rather than in the global namespace and, thus, help in cleaner management of the signals. We created two signals where the intent of the use of both is clear by their names.

Then, we need to create subscribers to these signals and attach functions to them. For this, the `add_index_to_es()` methods have to be removed, and new functions on the global scope have to be created:

```
def add_product_index_to_es(sender, product):
    es.index('catalog', 'product', {
        'name': product.name,
        'category': product.category.name
    })
    es.refresh('catalog')

product_created.connect(add_product_index_to_es, app)

def add_category_index_to_es(sender, category):
    es.index('catalog', 'category', {
        'name': category.name,
    })
    es.refresh('catalog')

category_created.connect(add_category_index_to_es, app)
```

In the preceding code snippet, we created subscribers to the signals created earlier using `.connect()`. This method accepts the function that should be called when the event occurs; it also accepts the sender as an optional argument. The `app` object is provided as the sender because we do not want our function to be called every time the event is triggered anywhere in any application. This specifically holds true in the case of extensions, which can be used by multiple applications. The function that gets called by the receiver gets the sender as the first argument, which defaults to none if the sender is not provided. We provided the product/category as the second argument for which the record needs to be added to the Elasticsearch index.

Now, we just need to emit the signal that can be caught by the receiver. This needs to be done in `views.py`. For this, we just need to remove the calls to the `add_index_to_es()` methods and replace them with the `.send()` methods:

```
from my_app.catalog.models import product_created, category_created


def create_product():
    #... normal product creation as always ...#
    db.session.commit()
    product_created.send(app, product=product)
    # product.add_index_to_es()
    #... normal process as always ...#
```

Do the same in the `create_category()` method as well.

How it works...

Whenever a product is created, the `product_created` signal is emitted, with the `app` object as the sender and the product as the keyword argument. This is then caught in `models.py`, and the `add_product_index_to_es()` function is called, which adds the document to the catalog index.

See also

▶ The *Full-text search with Elasticsearch* recipe for background information on this recipe

▶ Refer to `https://pypi.python.org/pypi/blinker`

▶ Refer to `http://flask.pocoo.org/docs/0.10/signals/#core-signals`

▶ Signals provided by Flask-SQLAlchemy can be found at `https://pythonhosted.org/Flask-SQLAlchemy/signals.html`

Using caching with your application

Caching becomes an important and integral part of any web application when scaling or increasing the response time of your application becomes a question. Caching is the first thing that is implemented in these cases. Flask, by itself, does not provide any caching support by default, but Werkzeug does. Werkzeug has some basic support to cache with multiple backends, such as Memcached and Redis.

Getting ready

We will install a Flask extension called Flask-Cache, which simplifies the process of caching a lot:

```
$ pip install Flask-Cache
```

We will use our catalog application for this purpose and implement caching for some methods.

How to do it...

First, we need to initialize `Cache` to work with our application. This is done in the application's configuration, that is, `my_app/__init__.py`:

```
from flask.ext.cache import Cache

cache = Cache(app, config={'CACHE_TYPE': 'simple'})
```

Here, we used `simple` as the `Cache` type where the cache is stored in the memory. This is not advised for production environments. For production, we should use something such as Redis, Memcached, filesystem cache, and so on. Flask-Cache supports all of them with a couple more backends.

Next, we need to add caching to our methods; this is pretty simple to implement. We just need to add a `@cache.cached(timeout=<time in seconds>)` decorator to our view methods. A simple target can be the list of categories (we will do this in `views.py`):

```
from my_app import cache

@catalog.route('/categories')
@cache.cached(timeout=120)
def categories():
    # Fetch and display the list of categories
```

This way of caching stores the value of the output of this method in the cache in the form of a key-value pair, with the key as the request path.

How it works...

After adding the preceding code, to check whether the cache works as expected, first fetch the list of categories by pointing the browser to `http://127.0.0.1:5000/categories`. This will save a key-value pair for this URL in the cache. Now, create a new category quickly and navigate back to the same category list page. You will notice that the newly added category is not listed. Wait for a couple of minutes and then reload the page. The newly added category will be shown now. This is because the first time the category list was cached, it expired after 2 minutes, that is, 120 seconds.

This might seem to be a fault with the application, but in the case of large applications, this becomes a boon where the hits to the database are reduced, and the overall application experience improves. Caching is usually implemented for those handlers whose results do not get updated frequently.

There's more...

Many of us might think that such caching will fail in the case of a single category or product page, where each record has a separate page. The solution to this is **memoization**. It is similar to cache with the difference that it stores the result of a method in the cache along with the information on the parameters passed. So, when a method is created with the same parameters multiple times, the result is loaded from the cache rather than making a database hit. Implementing memoization is again quite simple:

```
@catalog.route('/product/<id>')
@cache.memoize(120)
def product(id):
    # Fetch and display the product
```

Now, if we call a URL, say `http://127.0.0.1:5000/product/1` in our browser, the first time it will be loaded after making calls to the database. However, the next time, if we make the same call, the page will be loaded from the cache. On the other hand, if we open another product, say, `http://127.0.0.1:5000/product/2`, then it will be loaded after fetching the product details from the database.

See also

▶ Read more about Flask-Cache at `https://pythonhosted.org/Flask-Cache/`
▶ Read more about memoization at `http://en.wikipedia.org/wiki/Memoization`

E-mail support for Flask applications

The ability to send e-mails is usually one of the most basic functions of any web application. It is usually easy to implement with any application. With Python-based applications, it is also quite simple to implement with the help of smtplib. In the case of Flask, this is further simplified by an extension called **Flask-Mail**.

Getting ready

Flask-Mail can be easily installed via `pip`:

```
$ pip install Flask-Mail
```

Let's take a simple case where en e-mail will be sent to a catalog manager in the application whenever a new category is added.

How to do it...

First, we need to instantiate the `Mail` object in our application's configuration, that is, `my_app/__init__.py`:

```
from flask_mail import Mail

app.config['MAIL_SERVER'] = 'smtp.gmail.com'
app.config['MAIL_PORT'] = 587
app.config['MAIL_USE_TLS'] = True
app.config['MAIL_USERNAME'] = 'gmail_username'
app.config['MAIL_PASSWORD'] = 'gmail_password'
app.config['MAIL_DEFAULT_SENDER'] = ('Sender name', 'sender email')
mail = Mail(app)
```

Also, we need to do some configuration to set up the e-mail server and sender account. The preceding code is a sample configuration for Gmail accounts. Any SMTP server can be set up like this. There are several other options provided; they can be looked up in the Flask-Mail documentation at `https://pythonhosted.org/Flask-Mail`.

How it works...

To send an e-mail on category creation, we need to make the following changes in `views.py`:

```
from my_app import mail
from flask_mail import Message

@catalog.route('/category-create', methods=['GET', 'POST'])
def create_category():
    # ... Create category ... #
    db.session.commit()
    message = Message(
        "New category added",
        recipients=['some-receiver@domain.com']
    )
    message.body = 'New category "%s" has been created' %
      category.name
    mail.send(message)
    # ... Rest of the process ... #
```

Here, a new e-mail will be sent to the list of recipients from the default sender configuration that we created.

There's more...

Now, let's assume that we need to send a large e-mail with a lot of HTML content. Writing all this in our Python file will make the overall code ugly and unmanageable. A simple solution to this is to create templates and render their content while sending e-mails. I created two templates: one for the HTML content and one simply for text content.

The `category-create-email-text.html` template will look like this:

```
A new category has been added to the catalog.

The name of the category is {{ category.name }}.
Click on the URL below to access the same:
{{ url_for('catalog.category', id=category.id, _external = True) }}

This is an automated email. Do not reply to it.
```

The `category-create-email-html.html` template will look like this:

```
<p>A new category has been added to the catalog.</p>

<p>The name of the category is <a href="{{ url_for('catalog.category',
id=category.id, _external = True) }}">
    <h2>{{ category.name }}</h2>
  </a>.
</p>

<p>This is an automated email. Do not reply to it.</p>
```

After this, we need to modify our procedure of creating e-mail messages that we did earlier in the `views.py` file:

```
message.body = render_template(
    "category-create-email-text.html",
    category=category
)
message.html = render_template(
    "category-create-email-html.html",
    category=category
)
```

See also

▶ Read the next recipe, *Understanding asynchronous operations*, to see how we can delegate the time-consuming e-mail sending process to an asynchronous thread and speed up our application

Understanding asynchronous operations

Some of the operations in a web application can be time-consuming and make the overall application feel slow for the user, even though it's not actually slow. This decreases the user experience significantly. To deal with this, the simplest way to implement the asynchronous execution of operations is with the help of threads. In this recipe, we will implement it using the `thread` and `threading` libraries of Python. The `threading` library is simply an interface over `thread`; it provides more functionality and hides things that are normally not used by users.

Getting ready

We will use the application from the *E-mail support for Flask applications* recipe. Many of us will have noticed that while the e-mail is being sent, the application waits for the whole process to finish, which is actually unnecessary. E-mail sending can be easily done in the background, and our application can become available to the user instantaneously.

How to do it...

Doing an asynchronous execution with the `thread` library is very simple. Just add the following code to `views.py`:

```python
import thread

def send_mail(message):
    with app.app_context():
        mail.send(message)

# Replace the line below in create_category()
#mail.send(message)
# by
thread.start_new_thread(send_mail, (message,))
```

As you can see, the sending of an e-mail happens in a new thread, which sends the message as a parameter to the newly created method. We need to create a new `send_mail()` method because our e-mail templates contain `url_for`, which can be executed only inside an application context; this won't be available in the newly created thread by default.

Alternatively, sending an e-mail can also be done using the `threading` library:

```python
from threading import Thread

# Replace the previously added line in create_category() by
new_thread = Thread(target=send_mail, args=[message])
new_thread.start()
```

Effectively, the same thing happens as earlier but the `threading` library provides the flexibility of starting the thread whenever needed instead of creating and starting the thread at the same time.

How it works...

It is pretty simple to observe how this works. Compare the performance of this type of execution with the application in the previous recipe, *E-mail support for Flask applications*. You will notice that the application is more responsive. Another way can be to monitor the debug logs, where the newly created category's page will load before the e-mail is sent.

Working with Celery

Celery is a task queue for Python. Earlier, there used to be an extension to integrate Flask and Celery, but with Celery 3.0, it became obsolete. Now, Celery can be directly used with Flask by just using a bit of configuration. In the *Understanding asynchronous operations* recipe, we implemented asynchronous processing to send an e-mail. In this recipe, we will implement it using Celery.

Getting ready

Celery can be installed simply from PyPI:

```
$ pip install celery
```

To make Celery work with Flask, we will need to modify our Flask app config file a bit. Here, we will use Redis as the broker (thanks to its simplicity).

We will use the application from the previous recipe and implement Celery in it.

How to do it...

The first thing that we need to do is a bit of configuration in the application's configuration file, that is, `my_app/__init__.py`:

```
from celery import Celery

app.config.update(
    CELERY_BROKER_URL='redis://localhost:6379',
    CELERY_RESULT_BACKEND='redis://localhost:6379'
)

def make_celery(app):
    celery = Celery(
```

```
        app.import_name, broker=app.config['CELERY_BROKER_URL']
    )
    celery.conf.update(app.config)
    TaskBase = celery.Task
    class ContextTask(TaskBase):
        abstract = True
        def __call__(self, *args, **kwargs):
            with app.app_context():
                return TaskBase.__call__(self, *args, **kwargs)
    celery.Task = ContextTask
    return celery
```

The preceding snippet comes directly from the Flask website and can be used as is in your application in most cases:

```
celery = make_celery(app)
```

To run the Celery process, execute the following command:

```
$ celery worker -b redis://localhost:6379 --app=my_app.celery -l INFO
```

 Make sure that Redis is also running on the broker URL, as specified in the configuration.

Here, -b points to the broker, and –app points to the celery object that is created in the configuration file.

Now, we just need to use this celery object in our views.py file to send e-mails asynchronously:

```
from my_app import celery

@celery.task()
def send_mail(message):
    with app.app_context():
        mail.send(message)

# Add this line wherever the email needs to be sent
send_mail.apply_async((message,))
```

We add the @celery.task decorator to any method that we wish to be used as a Celery task. The Celery process will detect these methods automatically.

How it works...

Now, when we create a category and an e-mail is sent, we can see a task being run on the Celery process logs, which will look like this:

```
[2014-08-28 01:16:47,365: INFO/MainProcess] Received task: my_app.
catalog.views.send_mail[d2ca07ae-6b47-4b76-9935-17b826cdc340]
```

```
[2014-08-28 01:16:55,695: INFO/MainProcess] Task my_app.catalog.
views.send_mail[d2ca07ae-6b47-4b76-9935-17b826cdc340] succeeded in
8.329121886s: None
```

See also

- ▶ Refer to the *Understanding asynchronous operations* recipe to see how threads can be used for various purposes, in our case, to send e-mails

- ▶ Read more about Celery at `http://docs.celeryproject.org/en/latest/index.html`

Index

Instant Flask Web Development

ISBN: 978-1-78216-962-8   Paperback: 78 pages

Tap into Flask to build a complete application in a style that you control

1. Learn something new in an Instant! A short, fast, focused guide delivering immediate results.

2. Build a small but complete web application with Python and Flask.

3. Explore the basics of web page layout using Twitter Bootstrap and jQuery.

4. Get to know how to validate data entry using HTML forms and WTForms.

Learning Python Design Patterns

ISBN: 978-1-78328-337-8   Paperback: 100 pages

A practical and fast-paced guide exploring Python design patterns

1. Explore the Model-View-Controller pattern and learn how to build a URL shortening service.

2. All design patterns use a real-world example that can be modified and applied in your software.

3. No unnecessary theory! The book consists of only the fundamental knowledge that you need to know.

Please check **www.PacktPub.com** for information on our titles

Python Data Visualization Cookbook

ISBN: 978-1-78216-336-7   Paperback: 280 pages

Over 60 recipes that will enable you to learn how to create attractive visualizations using Python's most popular libraries

1. Learn how to set up an optimal Python environment for data visualization.

2. Understand topics such as importing data for visualization and formatting data for visualization.

3. Understand the underlying data and how to use the right visualizations.

Mastering Python Regular Expressions

ISBN: 978-1-78328-315-6   Paperback: 110 pages

Leverage regular expressions in Python even for the most complex features

1. Explore the workings of regular expressions in Python.

2. Learn all about optimizing regular expressions using RegexBuddy.

3. Full of practical and step-by-step examples, tips for performance, and solutions for performance-related problems faced by users all over the world.

Please check **www.PacktPub.com** for information on our titles

Made in the USA
Lexington, KY
30 July 2015